Cover design: Verla Kay

Printed and bound in the United States of America

ISBN 978-0-9717905-2-0

With all my love to three beautiful cousins, Carol, Sheryl and Pat —
shown here in my favorite picture of them when they were young.

Wings Forever

by

Verla Kay

Wings Forever

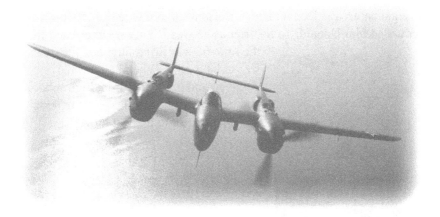

1

Being a fighter pilot during WWII was an extremely difficult occupation — fraught with danger — not only from enemy planes and anti-aircraft batteries but also from multiple equipment failures. While many thousands of feet above the ground and miles into enemy territory, a dangerous situation could become deadly at any moment and a pilot's instinctive reaction was often the only thing between him and a fiery death.

WWII pilots were a close-knit band of men; they stuck together and supported each other like there would be no tomorrow.

And for many of them, there *was* no tomorrow.

---

1 Image of a P-38 Lightning -- like the one Donn flew in the war

Part One - The Beginning

His legal name was Donald Bruce Deisenroth, but woe to anyone who ever called him Donald. To his friends he was Donn (or Dutch) and from

the time he was just a little boy his passion was to be a pilot. When he'd turned eighteen and graduated from high school he knew it was time to leave his parents' home and learn to fly. But how?

The answer?

On July 22, 1940, he joined the Army Air Corps,[2] a branch of the military that later became the Air Force.

When enlisted he was 18 4/12 years of age and by occupation a Student He had Hazel eyes, Brown hair, Fair complexion, and was 5 feet 8½ inches in height.

---

2 The Department of the Air Force was formed on September 18, 1947, after WWII had ended. Until this new department of the military was created, Army pilots were part of the Army Air Corps.

Donald (Donn) B. Deisenroth

After completing basic training, Donn attended Air Corps Technical School (ACTS) in Lowry Field,[3] Colorado.

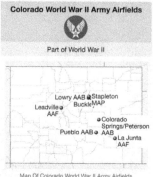

Map Of Colorado World War II Army Airfields

3 The city of Denver purchased a tuberculosis hospital (the Agnes Phipps Memorial Sanatorium) for an airfield after a 1935 municipal bond vote. On August 27,1937, the sanatorium grounds were converted into a military airfield. In February 1938, the airfield being installed adjacent to Fairmont Cemetery was assigned to the Air Corps Technical School, turning the Denver branch of the Army Air Corps into an Army post of 880 acres.

At 7:48 AM on December 7, 1941, Donn's world changed — forever. People all over the United States woke up to newspaper extras[4] and radios blaring about a deadly attack on Pearl Harbor that had been carried out by the Japanese, catapulting the United States and all of the men in the armed forces into WWII.

On that eventful day Donn's status changed in the Army Air Corps from an insignificant pilot-in-training into a valuable future asset — a fighter pilot that the military fully intended to use to help defeat the enemy in this terrible world war that had so suddenly been forced upon the United States of America.

When 360 Japanese planes attacked Pearl Harbor on that infamous day, five battleships sank, 2403 Americans died and 200 planes were destroyed. People all over the United States were in a state of shock.

---

4 Radios, newspapers and word of mouth were the primary means of getting news in 1941. For up-to-the-minute news, people huddled around their radios. Newspapers only came out once a day except in extremely newsworthy cases — like after the attack on Pearl Harbor — when many newspapers printed an "extra" paper in addition to their regular daily paper.

Pilots were instantly in great demand and Donn's focus immediately turned to "The War." His plans for the future had changed overnight; now he didn't just want to be a pilot, he wanted to be a *fighter* pilot so he could help the United States beat the Axis powers.[5]

His first Army post was in Santa Maria, California, at the Hancock-College of Aeronautics, where he finally got to fly his first plane.

It was a Stearman[6] PT-13 biplane with two seats in it — one for the student pilot and one for the instructor. Stearman planes had two sets of wings, one above the other — and they were extremely sturdy — ideal for training new pilots.

---

5 WWII officially began when Great Britain and France declared war against Germany on September 3, 1939. But the United States was not a full participant of the war until after the bombing of Pearl Harbor, when President Franklin D. Roosevelt announced that the United States had declared war on Japan and the other Axis powers — Germany, Italy, Hungary, Romania and Bulgaria. The United States was now formally part of the Allied forces of WWII — including Britain, France, USSR (Russia), Australia, Belgium, Brazil, Canada, China, Denmark, Greece, Netherlands, New Zealand, Norway, Poland, South Africa, and Yugoslavia.

6 Approximately half of all of the US military pilots who fought in WWII received their initial flight training in Stearman PT-13 Kaydet biplanes. 8,430 of these planes were built before manufacturing ended in 1944. No other biplane was ever produced in such numbers.

In 1939, the Luftwaffe (Germany's aerial warfare branch during WWII) ruled the skies over Europe, but the United States had few pilots and no aviation training facilities. Between July 1, 1939, and June 30, 1944, more than 8,400 aviation cadets and student officers were trained at the Hancock College of Aeronautics. Donn was one of those students.

His very first flight was for 30 minutes on May, 30, 1942. He was now officially a student pilot — but he always had a qualified instructor flying with him. In this first page of Donn's flight log, there is only one column of flight times. Above that column is the word, "Dual," which indicated that two people were flying the plane -- the student and the instructor.

Donn learned quickly and his first solo flight (for 13 minutes) was just 22 days after he started learning to fly.

On the second page in Donn's flight log you can see how many minutes and/or hours he flew with an instructor (the times listed in the left-hand column of his log book) and how much time he spent flying solo — by himself— without an instructor in the plane with him (the times listed in the right-hand column of his flight log).

He flew Stearman biplanes for another month before moving on to a more advanced trainer plane — A Vultee BT-13 Valiant. This single-engine plane has an all-metal low wing and fixed landing gear which does not retract into the plane while in flight; instead, the wheels are always down, allowing the plane to land at any time. Flight instruments and dual controls were standard equipment.

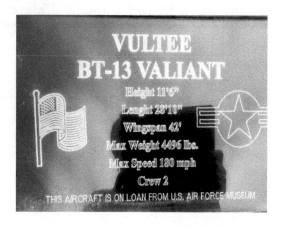

From September 1939, to the Summer of 1944, a total of 11,537 Vultees were built -- making this plane one of the most important American trainer aircraft of World War II.

Once Donn became experienced flying single-engine aircraft, he learned to fly a Curtiss-Wright AT-9 Jeep.

This was a twin-engined advanced trainer aircraft used by the United States to bridge the gap between single-engine trainers and twin-engined combat aircraft. It was a low-wing cantilever monoplane design, had retractable landing gear — wheels that disappeared up into the plane's fuselage (the body of the plane) when it was in the air — and it was powered by two engines, each with its own propeller.

Once he started flying more frequently, Donn often grumbled, "All I ever wanted was to be a pilot — that's why I joined the Army Air Corps — to fly planes. But after I'd joined and started flying, I discovered that even though they got less flying hours, it was the Navy pilots that got to fly all the best and newest airplanes. If I'd known that before I enlisted, I'd have joined the Navy instead of the Army!"

Donn was still a student pilot, stationed in Santa Maria, California, when he met a very special girl. As rebellious as Donn had been about attending church while living at home —it was totally ironic that it was while he and a group of his fellow flying trainees were attending a church service in Sacramento that Donn met his sweetheart, Norma. It was love at first sight and after a whirlwind romance they soon became engaged.

No one ever called Norma by her first name, Lois, because that was also her mother's and her niece's name. She went by Norma but her family most often called her, "Sis," and Donn sometimes called her, "Squirt."

Norma and her seven siblings are lined up by age. She is the youngest — on the far right.

Norma's parents didn't think much of Donn at first. They said, "He's a cocky little pilot!" And they didn't like the way he ordered her around.

But Norma didn't mind at all. She was happiest when Donn took charge and told her what to do, because she believed that women were expected to get married, obey their husbands without question, raise the children, cook and take care of the home while men made all the important decisions and supported their families. That's just the way it was in 1942.

Norma's best friend while she was growing up was her niece, Lois. Because all six of her sisters were older than Norma, several of them were old enough to be her mother, and she and her niece were almost the same age. They lived together much of the time, and did nearly everything together.

Lois and Norma on homemade wooden stilts when they were children

Norma

Lois

The next phase of Donn's training took place at ACTS Officer Candidate school, which focused on pilot and aircrew training, technical training and basic training of enlisted personnel.

Donn was so proud to be in the very first class of U.S. Army Air Corps flight officers to graduate from this school that he even had business cards printed to give to his friends.

Donald B. Deisenroth

FLIGHT OFFICER
ARMY OF THE UNITED STATES

This newspaper article mentioned one disadvantage Donn had of being one of these first officers to graduate from the ACTS Officer Candidate School.

FIRST FLIGHT OFFICER HERE ON FURLOUGH

So new is his army designation and so little known is his insignia that Donald B. Deisenroth of Pasadena is being looked upon as quite a "pioneer" among his home town friends. He was a member of the first class to be graduated as flight officers, U.S. Army Air Corps.

FIRST FLIGHT OFFICER HERE ON FURLOUGH

Home on a brief furlough before taking up assignment at a Glendale airport, he wears bars on his shoulders, similar to those of a lieutenant, only these bars are broken by a gold line through the center, causing the wearer no little merriment as he is eyed by others in the service.

"Our insignia is new," he said today, "no one knows whether to salute us or not." ....

....

<Donn> got his wings Dec. 3 .... <he> also got the new designation "flight officer, first class."

Out of the Glendale airport he will be flying P-38s until he gets into the "big show.[7]"

So new is his army designation and so little known is his insignia that Donald B. Deisenroth of Pasadena is being looked upon as quite a "pioneer" among his home town friends. He was a member of the first class to be graduated as flight officers, U. S. Army Air Corps.

Home on a brief furlough before taking up assignment at a Glendale airport, he wears bars on his shoulders, similar to those of a lieutenant, only these bars are broken by a gold line through the center, causing the wearer no little merriment as he is eyed by others in the service. "Our insignia is new," he said today, "no one knows whether to salute us or not."

Born in Pasadena, he is the son of J. B. Deisenroth of 829 North Los Robles Avenue. He secured most of his education at the Oakland Technical High School, enlisting in the Air Corps July 22, 1940. He studied at Santa Maria and LeMoore and got his wings Dec. 3 at Luke Field, Arizona—also the new designation "flight officer, first class." Out of the Glendale airport he will be flying P-38's until he gets into the "big show."

---

7 The "big show" was slang for a major military campaign

While Donn was studying hard and learning to fly, the war raged on in the South Pacific and in Europe.

On February 23, 1942, a Japanese submarine fired on coastal targets near Santa Barbara, California. Damage was minimal, but it resulted in widespread fear throughout the country. It reinforced the government's decision to round up all of the Japanese citizens of the United States — women, men and even the children — and force all of them to move into internment camps.

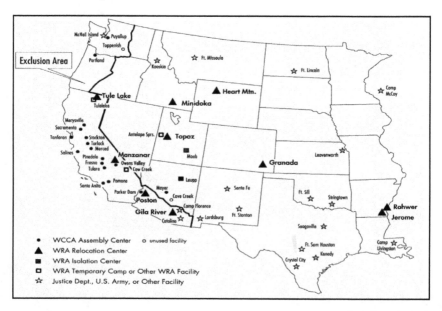

Japanese Americans had to leave their homes, their businesses, EVERY-THING, and live in fenced compounds like prisoners because people were afraid they might be loyal to Japan instead of the United States.

President Franklin D. Roosevelt authorized the deportation and incarceration with an Executive Order issued on February 19, 1942, allowing regional military commanders to designate "military areas" from which "any or all persons may be excluded." This power was used to declare that all people of Japanese ancestry were excluded from the entire West Coast, including all of California and much of Oregon, Washington and Arizona, except for those in government camps.

WESTERN DEFENSE COMMAND AND FOURTH ARMY
WARTIME CIVIL CONTROL ADMINISTRATION
Presidio of San Francisco, California
April 1, 1942

INSTRUCTIONS
TO ALL PERSONS OF
JAPANESE
ANCESTRY
Living in the Following Area:

All that portion of the City and County of San Francisco, State of California, lying generally west of the north-south line established by Junipero Serra Boulevard, Worchester Avenue, and Nineteenth Avenue, and lying generally north of the east-west line established by California Street, to the intersection of Market Street, and thence on Market Street to San Francisco Bay.

All Japanese persons, both alien and non-alien, will be evacuated from the above designated area by 12:00 o'clock noon Tuesday, April 7, 1942.

No Japanese person will be permitted to enter or leave the above described area after 8:00 a. m., Thursday, April 2, 1942, without obtaining special permission from the Provost Marshal at the Civil Control Station located at:
1701 Van Ness Avenue
San Francisco, California

The Civil Control Station is equipped to assist the Japanese population affected by this evacuation in the following ways:

1. Give advice and instructions on the evacuation.
2. Provide services with respect to the management, leasing, sale, storage or other disposition of most kinds of property including: real estate, business and professional equipment, buildings, household goods, boats, automobiles, livestock, etc.
3. Provide temporary residence elsewhere for all Japanese in family groups.
4. Transport persons and a limited amount of clothing and equipment to their new residence, as specified below.

The Following Instructions Must Be Observed:
1. A responsible member of each family, preferably the head of the family, or the person [...]
the property is held, and each individual living alone, will report [...]
structions. This must be done [...]
5:00 [...]

Between 110,000 and 120,000 Japanese Americans, many of whom lived on the West Coast, were evacuated from their homes and forcibly relocated into these camps during the spring of 1942.

The Supreme Court upheld the constitutionality of the removal, avoiding the issue of the incarceration of U.S. citizens without due process.

In 1980, many years after the war, President Jimmy Carter opened an investigation to determine whether the decision to put Japanese Americans into internment camps had been justified by the government. The Commission's report, titled "Personal Justice Denied," found little evidence of Japanese disloyalty at the time and concluded that the incarceration had been the product of racism.

Then, in 1988, President Ronald Reagan signed into law the Civil Liberties Act, which apologized for the internment on behalf of the U.S. government and authorized a payment of $20,000 to each individual camp survivor. The U.S. government eventually disbursed more than $1.6 billion in reparations to 82,219 Japanese Americans (and to their heirs) who had been interned.

Many things in the every day life of all of the citizens of the United States changed because of the war. It was definitely not "life as normal." Some regulations were put into effect even before the United States was catapulted into active participation in the war.

The government issued very strict blackout orders to civilians[8]. At night all windows were required to be completely covered with blackout curtains, cardboard or paint so no light could show through them. Streetlights were covered so that only a small light was cast straight downward.

Even automobile headlights were dimmed and covered with tape because enemy planes would have a harder time identifying targets at night if there were no lights helping them to know where the cities were.

---

8 Blackout regulations were imposed on September 1, 1939, even before the United States had entered the war.

Norma and Lois helped by walking around their neighborhood knocking on the doors of homes that didn't have their windows covered, reminding people inside of the dangers of letting their lights show.

One neighbor refused to cover his windows.

He yelled at them, "No one is going to tell ME what to do!"

And there was no way the girls could *make* the man cover his windows, so they had to walk away, shaking their heads, leaving him alone with his lights blaring out into the night. even though there were heavy legal penalties for people who disobeyed the government's order.

It wasn't long until Donn married Norma in Kings County, California, on September 5, 1942 — when he was 20 and she was 19.

Since they were both underage, (in those days you weren't legally an adult until you were 21) both of their fathers had to give written permission for them to be married.

Because of the war, gasoline was in short supply and travel was difficult for most people so only her father, her closest sister, Verla, and Donn's father witnessed them saying their vows.

Norma always felt sad that she had to get married in a black dress, but it was her best dress and because of the war, there wasn't time, money or material for her to have a fancy white wedding dress.

Shortly before her marriage to Donn, Norma was invited to play the violin in the Sacramento Symphony Orchestra (she was an extremely accomplished singer and violinist) but she turned down that job offer so she could marry Donn. Norma firmly believed a woman should not work outside of the home if she was married; instead, she intended to be a housewife, homemaker and — hopefully someday soon — a mother.

They sent a postcard to Norma's mother the day after they got married. Donn and Norma each wrote a message on it. The postcard reads as follows:

(from Donn) *Hello Mom, the knot was tied at 6:30pm yesterday, Sept. 5th. Must be kind of tough on you and your husband, losing 2 daughters in one day[9]. Or is it a relief? But we are HAPPY!* (and from Norma) *He says write, but I'm going to write a letter tomorrow and I can't think now anyhow — Tell everybody, "We dood it!" Love, Sis and Donn*

They sent another postcard the same day to one of Norma's sisters. Donn wrote on it, "*I'm sending your sister back. Do I get a refund?*" (He had a great sense of humor — and so did Norma. They laughed a lot together.)

---

9 Donn's mention of Norma's parents "losing two daughters in one day" referred to the fact that one of Norma's older sisters also got married on that same day.

There is always a period of adjustment when a person's living arrangements change (like when a person gets married) but during WWII it was especially challenging. Rationing began almost as soon as the United States was catapulted into WWII with tires, cars and typewriters, and these rationed items were soon followed by sugar, gasoline and bicycles.

As the war went on, many more items were rationed. Many things that were easy to obtain before the war were in short supply or impossible to buy during the war. Metal, nylon, silk, rubber and cooking oil were all needed in great quantities to make tanks, ships, airplanes, parachutes, grenades, bombs, guns, bullets and torpedoes, as well as uniforms and other items necessary for the men fighting for our country.

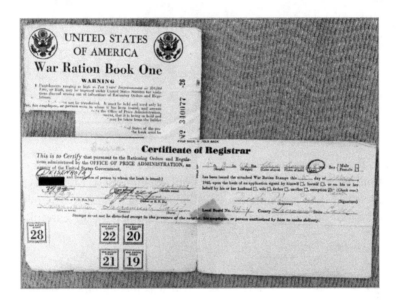

Ration stamp books, like this first one assigned to Norma on May 5th, 1942, were issued to people at home. Every person who lived in the United States received one ration stamp book — even newborn babies — and that one book had to last for several months. Civilians had to use the stamps in the book to buy things that were rationed and some things, like nylon stockings, couldn't be purchased at all.

If they ran out of stamps, they couldn't buy rationed items, no matter how much money they had or how badly the items were needed! Everyone was very careful to "ration" their stamps and plan ahead to make sure they had enough stamps to last until they got their next book. You can see that Norma's first ration stamp book had only five stamps left when her second book was issued.

Ration books changed after the first books of stamps were issued. In the first book Norma received, the stamps were just numbers. Later books had stamps for specific items.

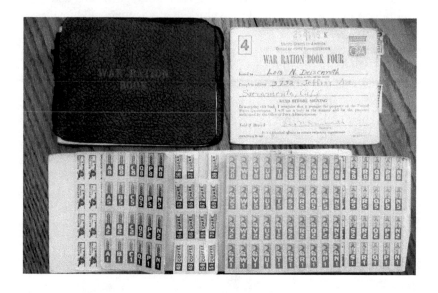

Norma's fourth ration book had a limited number of stamps in it for each kind of rationed item — coffee, sugar, flour, gasoline, etc. She always had the hardest time rationing her gasoline and sugar stamps. They were always the first ones to be used up unless she planned VERY carefully.

Another big change during the war was the amount of posters that were seen everywhere. They reminded people to conserve and ration carefully because that was one way civilians at home could help our soldiers.

People were encouraged to conserve and save in every way possible, so that needed resources of the country could be used in the war effort. One way to save was to plant a garden to grow your own food. These were called, "Victory Gardens." This poster reminded those at home that growing your own food could help with the war.

"Victory Gardens" were grown everywhere — in large fields, small plots of land and even in pots on porches. Growing your own food was one way to make sure there was enough to eat because you didn't need ration stamps for food you grew yourself.

Other posters encouraged people to buy war bonds and stamps to help finance the war.

$5 (highest denomination)
"Minuteman" War Savings Stamp
(sepia) 1942

10¢ (lowest denomination)
"Minuteman" US War Savings Stamp
(rose red) 1942

War bonds were available from $25 through $1000 and people bought them at 75% of their face value. For example, people would pay $18.75 for a $25 war bond. When it matured in ten years, they would turn the bond in and get $25. War stamps were also available for between 10¢ and $5 per stamp. They were collected in special albums and when an album was full, it could be exchanged for a war bond. 10¢ and 25¢ stamps were very popular with children.

In those days, women always wore silk or nylon stockings when they went out, but the government needed every bit of silk and nylon it could get to manufacture parachutes, tire cords, ropes, aircraft fuel tanks, shoe laces, mosquito netting and hammocks to aid in the U.S.'s national defense, so nylon was severely rationed and channeled into war efforts.

Because nylon was in such high demand by the military, most women donated their stockings to the war effort and once they were gone, they couldn't get any more. Stockings weren't made like they are today — there was a seam up the back of the stockings and women were very careful to keep that seam straight so their legs would look attractive. Without any stockings to wear women would sometimes very carefully draw a "seam line" up the backs of their legs with an eyebrow pencil.

When Norma wanted to look like she was wearing stockings, Lois would help her by drawing her seam lines, since it was almost impossible to get the lines straight unless you had a friend helping. It wasn't fun and was too much work to do very often.

All kinds of things were collected to be made into planes, tanks, bombs and parachutes for the war effort. In those days they called it "collecting scrap." (Today we call it recycling.)

REMEMBER —
IT IS THE PATRIOTIC DUTY OF EVERY AMERICAN CITIZEN TO SEE TO IT THAT ALL SCRAP GETS INTO THE FIGHT!

Young children helped, too, by holding scrap drives, then buying war stamps with the pennies they earned. Anything and everything was collected for the war effort. Children even donated their beloved metal toys to be melted down to make tanks and planes.

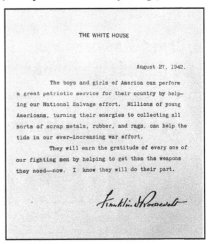

THE WHITE HOUSE

August 27, 1942.

The boys and girls of America can perform a great patriotic service for their country by helping our National Salvage effort. Millions of young Americans, turning their energies to collecting all sorts of scrap metals, rubber, and rags, can help the tide in our ever-increasing war effort.

They will earn the gratitude of every one of our fighting men by helping to get them the weapons they need—now. I know they will do their part.

Franklin D. Roosevelt

A lot of rubber was needed and old tires were very much in demand.

Even the grease left over from cooking was saved and turned over to the government. It was used to make glycerin which was then used to make explosives — like bombs!

V-Mail, short for Victory Mail, was used by the military during World War II. It involved the microfilming of specially designed letter sheets. Instead of using valuable cargo space to ship whole letters overseas, microfilmed copies were sent instead and then they were "blown up" (printed in full size) at an overseas facility before being delivered to military personnel.

Using V-Mail meant that thousands of tons of shipping space could be used for war materials instead of for paper letters. The 37 mail bags required to carry 150,000 one-page letters could be replaced by a single mail sack. The weight of that same amount of mail was reduced dramatically from 2,575 pounds to a mere 45 pounds.

Letters were written on special V-Mail letter-sheets, which were a combination of both letter and envelope. The letter-sheets were constructed and gummed so as to fold into a uniform and distinctively marked envelope. The user wrote the message in the limited space provided, added the name and address of the recipient, folded the form, affixed any needed postage and then mailed the letter. (Fighting men in the military didn't have to pay postage.)

V-Mail correspondence was then reduced to thumbnail size on micro-film. The rolls of film were sent to prescribed designations for developing at a receiving station near the addressee.

Finally, individual facsimiles of the letter-sheets were reproduced — sometimes at about one quarter of the original size — and the mail was then delivered to the addressee.

This is the first V-Mail letter Donn wrote — while he was on his transport ship. Note that the date has been censored — cut out of the letter. The military didn't want the enemy to find anything out about the ships that were transporting the men to the fighting lines (also known as "the front").

10

Dear Mother, Dad, and Aileen[11],

We have been at sea 12 days now and for the last few days it has been quite rough. It hasn't bothered me much, except for the first day. I never did get sick enough to throw anything up but I felt awfully sick that first day. We should land in another four days if all goes well. I don't know where I'm going for sure but I'm awfully certain it'll be where we thought I was going. Maybe I'll meet Fielding Wetherford[12] if he's really there.

We ran into a large school of porpoises today. It was fun watching them. There were hundreds of them jumping out of the water, etc. By the time you get this you will probably already have gotten my new A.P.O.[13] which I don't know yet. I think of you all a lot. I guess I've thought of you every night as I lay in bed. We sleep in our clothes now, with full canteens, and lifebelts, on or near us, as we are in the sub zone.

I hope you are all well. Be sure to write to me, and don't forget to write to Norma. Don't worry about me, as I won't take any unnecessary chances.

With lots of love,

Your son, Donn B.D.

---

10 This is one of the ships that transported troops during the war. It is unknown what ship Donn was on.

11 Aileen was Donn's older sister — his only sibling

12 Fielding was a buddy of Donn's from his early training days

13 A.P.O. is an Army Post Office military address

There were posters everywhere, reminding people to censor what they said so the enemy wouldn't learn about troop movements, etc.

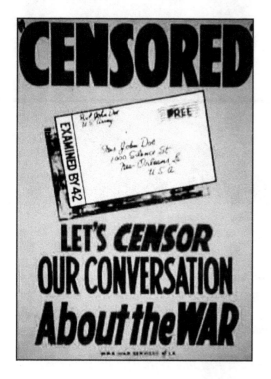

This letter from Donn was censored so much, there's almost nothing left of it!

What can be read says, "*March 24, 1943*

<censored>

We'll get mail about once a month here. That's not very often. Oh what I wouldn't give for a quart of milk — even for a glass of good old milk.

I'm tired waiting around doing nothing. <censored> on the boat and four days here now.

All the news that we have gotten as to the P-38s fighting qualities has...

<The remainder of this letter is missing.>

Part Two - At the Front

Donn was part of the very first group of American pilots to fly P-38 fighter planes out of North Africa into Italy during WWII.

Undated letter to Donn's Parents

I miss you folks – most of all my darling wife. I look at the pictures that I have of Norma quite often.

Just got my baggage here this morning. Am I glad to get it. Oh, boy. You'd give anything, I'm sure, to see me now, if you only knew what I look like. I haven't shaved for weeks. I got a "blitz"[14] hair cut. The only hair I have is right on top of my bean[15] – oh boy. We had hash again last night and Spam again today.

What a life. Well, tell one and all "Hello" for me. S'all for now – your loving son, Donn B. Deisenroth

---

14 A blitz haircut was very short hair on top and shaved around the sides
15 His bean was his head

Letter from Donn written April 15, 1943 (Date determined by examining his flight log book.)

DATE: "I have no idea – don't care."

Dear Mom, Dad & Aileen,

Just a few lines to let you know that I'm still alive and unhappy in this stinking place. I finally flew an airplane – Whee! – I flew one hour yesterday in a P-38 and I'm supposed to fly tomorrow. Hope so.

Only half of us are left now. The half with the most hours are up at the front. I'll probably be in action by the time this letter reaches you. I hope.

I guess you know the Axis[16] are getting thoroughly beaten over here. I hope by the time this letter reaches you we'll have kicked them out of Africa. I only hope I get in on this second Dunkirk[17]. When they try to evacuate, I imagine we'll be bothering them "slightly."

In case you're wondering about the kind of airplanes we have here, I can truthfully say there are nothing but the best here. Some models here are later models than I flew in the "States."

I have a lot to tell you about what Africa is like and how the people and their customs, etc. are, but I'll tell you all that in detail when I come home for Christmas. Everyone seems to think the war over here will be over by then. I hope so, too!

If it weren't for Norma I think I wouldn't mind Foreign Service much but I still can't sleep nights thinking about her. I hate WAR! Yeah! Already.

Hoping you're all well and happy.

I remain – your homesick son,

Donn

---

16 In World War II the Axis powers (Germany, Italy, Japan, Hungary, Romania, and Bulgaria) fought versus the Allies (United States of America, Britain, France, USSR, Australia, Belgium, Brazil, Canada, China, Denmark, Greece, Netherlands, New Zealand, Norway, Poland, South Africa, and Yugoslavia).
17 Dunkirk is "a period of crisis or emergency when drastic measures must be enforced."

Picture labeled, "The Boys." Donn is in the back row, the fourth guy from the left.

Letter written to Donn's parents – April 26, 1943

Hello, All,

Well, I finally got here. I'm at the front. I'll be in action in a couple of days. Just got here today. I like it here. Still live in a tent without a floor, but we have a stove so it's pretty good....

Well, not much more to say – oh, yeah – I just remembered. When I landed the other day my nose wheel fell off and then the nose wheel strut broke off. I slid down the field on the ship's nose. I had belly tanks, too – half full of gas – but luckily no fire. I didn't even get scratched.

Don't tell Norma – I didn't.

Lots of love to you all,

Donn

18

18 Two men, loading the guns of a P-38 in Africa.

Letter – May 2, 1943

Dear Mom, Dad, Sis and All,

I forgot to tell you in my last letter that I met up with my friend, Fielding. He's still a second Lieutenant, but he's due to be promoted soon. He works (if you can call it that) behind a desk now. He flies an AT-6 enough each month to get his flying pay. He really has a soft job. A very great chance of (him) being a captain in a few months and nothing at all dangerous about his work.

I'd rather have my job. I think I'm through training here now. I may get to go on my first mission tomorrow or next day. Got sunburnt today. Awfully hot.

Guess I never told you that I was out with five Australian flyers one night. I called them Aussie and they called me Yank and we had quite a good time. Well, I hope this finds you all in good health. WRITE OFTEN! Love, Donn

From Donn's Flight Diary[19] - May 4, 1943

Went on first mission yesterday. A weather mission. Purpose is to report weather conditions over targets – Sicily, Sardinia, Tunis, Bizerte, etc. Overcast from 300 feet to 11,000 feet. More clouds at 12,500 feet.

Took off at 10:15. Got to Bone and Shawn's generator went out, so both of us came right back. Took off again at 12:15. Didn't have to go to trail level[20] because weather was so bad that we could easily lose any Jerries[21] that might spot us. So after passing over Bone 2nd time, we hit the deck[22], because Jerries' radar isn't any good below 100 feet.

19 This is the first page of Donn's "makeshift" flight diary
20 "Trail level" is flying very close to the ground – under the enemy's radar.
21 The American fliers called the German fighters, "Jerries."
22 To "hit the deck" was to quickly dive down very low to the ground.

Sneaked right into Tunis Harbor within a few miles of the city itself. I'll bet they didn't even have any idea that 2 enemy planes were in that vicinity.

Ran into some heavier stuff (*clouds*), had to go on instruments. Got screwed up somehow. Needle on one side, ball on the other. Somehow got over almost on my back at 100 feet (*above the ocean*). Happened to see water through a break in the stuff and rolled out just in time. If it hadn't been for that break in the stuff, I guess I'd have gone right on in.[23] Scared me pretty badly.

Watched gyro horizon like cat watches a mouse until I broke out of it (*the clouds*) at 11,000 feet. Sweat was running down my nose and chin and my hands were dripping. Went on oxygen and called for homing. Homing didn't work. Belly tank ran dry, switched to main tanks, which were almost empty. Reserve tank gauges read almost empty.

Over strange country in ship almost out of gas, sitting on top of 11,000 feet overcast is no fun. Figured I'd have to bail out. Wouldn't try to make a letdown over strange terrain in that soup. That's what Clark tried to do. He hit a mountain. [24]

Suddenly found a hole. Dropped the bottom out[25] and went through. Leveled out at 200 feet just under overcast. Didn't recognize terrain. Getting dangerously low on fuel. Spotted a large plowed field. Buzzed[26] it and it looked okay, so dropped my gear and landed. Nose wheel strut broke. Slid a few feet on the nose. Very little damage. Me unhurt. Walked into camp at 21:30. Fellows were mighty glad to see me. Said they figured I had hit a mountain trying to make a letdown. Total flight was a little over 5 hours. My rear end was mighty sore![27]

---

23 "...gone right on in" meant he would have crashed into the ocean.
24 P-38s had a very complicated instrument panel. It took a lot of skill to fly a Lightning.
25 To "drop the bottom out" means to dive a plane straight down
26 "To Buzz" means to fly quickly once over an area of land in order to check its condition – what kinds of obstacles might be in or around it, etc.
27 P-38 fighter planes had bare metal seats in them with no padding.

From Donn's Flight Diary - May 9, 1943

Went on second mission today. Escorting B-17s to bomb Polerma, Sicily.

Today's show was biggest show yet. 130 B-17s and 100 P-38s. Took off at 0800 hours. Got out two hours and was just off Sicily when we started to climb. Found leak in left engine supercharger line.

Couldn't get enough manifold pressure to stay in formation. Had to return. Logged 4 hours.

Dinswiddie, Benton, Pyle, White, Curaan, Connors, Kedding and Snyder have been killed now.

From Donn's Flight Diary - May 10, 1943

Entered hospital last night after mission. Have Yellow Jaundice[28].

---

28 Yellow Jaundice was a fairly common occurrence during the war. In adults it can be caused by the Hepatitis virus. Its flu-like symptoms can include fever, chills, dark colored urine, clay-like stools, and abdominal pain. The skin changes to a yellow color, including the whites of the eyes, because of a buildup of bilirubin, a yellow-orange bile pigment which is secreted by the liver. Bilirubin is formed from the breakdown of red blood cells.

Letter - May 13, 1943

Dear Mother, Dad, Aileen and All, Everybody here is quite happy about our complete victory in North Africa.[29] People in the States can't realize, I suppose, what it has meant. It is the victorious ending of a campaign, in which the Allies started out in an apparent losing fight. It has been a fight in which the Axis pitted their strength against that of the Allies, and the Axis continually lost; until at the end they were so bitterly defeated that they made no attempt at a last stand.

What happens next is just everybody's question. But I say that no matter what it is, the Axis had better take heed, for we have done it before, we have just done it now, and we will do it again and again and again, if necessary. I'll bet the morale of the British people and troops, as well as that of the American troops, has been boosted 100% by this victory.

I hope you are all well. I am fine, feeling better every day. Which reminds me – I don't think I told you. I have been in the hospital for about 4 days now. I've got Yellow Jaundice. I'll be out in about 10 days. Miss you all and hope that you are writing regularly and OFTEN. No mail from you as yet. Give my regards to all. Your loving son, Donn

From Donn's Flight Diary - May 21, 1943

Got out of hospital this morning, but can't fly for a week at least.

From Donn's Flight Diary - May 28, 1943

Bryson disappeared yesterday. Nobody knows what happened to him. He turned back from the mission and never got home. Lost Captain Stentz and Hall and Bennet and Frieng. One of them bailed out and they think two of them bellied in[30]. So they figure that three of them may be alive but prisoners.

---

29 The Tunisia Campaign (also known as the Battle of Tunisia) was a series of battles that took place in Tunisia during the North African Campaign of the Second World War between Axis and Allied forces. The battles began with initial success by the German and Italian forces, but the massive supply and numerical superiority of the Allies led to the Axis's complete defeat with the fall of Tunis on May 12,1943, the day before Donn wrote this letter to his parents and his sister. Over 230,000 German and Italian troops were taken as prisoners of war.

30 Bellied in is when a plane lands or goes into the water on its belly without any wheels touching the ground.

One of them is gone for sure, though. He went straight in. Don't know which one it was. Hope it wasn't Hall. He has a wife and baby.

From Donn's Flight Diary - May 30, 1943

Went on dive-bombing mission to northern Sardinia. A couple of Macchi's[31] jumped us, but one of them was immediately shot down and the other vamoosed. Logged 5 1/2 hours. Had to land at Bone to refuel.

From Donn's Flight Diary - May 31, 1943

Went on dive-bombing mission today and got jumped by eight ME109s[32]. Have never been so scared in all my life. Wasn't on the ball and lost flight leader. It was my fault. That's when I got scared – when I found I was alone. Elkin got shot up – plane on fire, flew straight into mountain and blew up. Must have been dead or unconscious before he hit. Loder hit the ocean doing about 400 and the plane just broke up into little pieces. He was either wounded or just misjudged his altitude, I think. Logged 3 hours and 10 minutes. From now on I'm going to stay in formation if I have to split a gut doing it.

Letter written June 2, 1943

Dear Mom & Dad,

I was awfully glad to hear from you both yesterday. So it makes YOUR heart skip a beat, huh, Dad, to think of a Jerry on my tail? Well – your heart has a right to skip a beat because mine beats three times as fast as normally when the Jerries are buzzing around. Really though, Dad and Mom, it is a frightening sight to see those Jerries coming down on you. At first you don't know what to do – you're in kind of a panic – then you start doing things and get control of yourself, sort of.

The first time I saw one coming down, I just about went crazy and then from then on I was too busy to think.

---

31 A Macchi was considered the best Italian fighter plane of WWII.
32 A German ME109 was considered to be one of the most advanced and dangerous fighter planes of WWII.

I'm sorry, but I can't tell you how many missions I've been on, or where to, or how much time I've got, but I can say that more than once I've been in the same part of the sky with Jerry fighters. It's no fun, either. Everything that happens, and everything that is done from the time you're jumped is done in split (and I do mean split) seconds.

The Germans have some wonderful fighter planes. The ME-109G and the FW-190 are the most dangerous. That FW-190 is really armored, too. I put lead from all five of my guns in a 190 one day. I was really pouring the lead into him, and I didn't see him go in.

German ships aren't like the Italian Zeros – one shot and "BLOOEY!" goes the Zero. The Italian pilots aren't near as aggressive, either. It's almost, (almost, I said) fun to fight them.

I'll quit for now. I hope that you and Mother are very well. With lots of love, Your son, Donn

This is a photograph of Donn with one of his flying buddies. Donn is on the right.

From Donn's Flight Diary - June 15, 1943

The last nine missions have been so uneventful that I haven't bothered to write up anything about them. That is, they were all uneventful except the June 11ᵗʰ mission to Pantelleria. We were patrolling north of the island, watching the invasion. Also there were "Spits" *(Spitfire planes),* P-39s, P-40s and Mustangs patrolling, covering the invasion.

We kept watching each flight of single engine fighters that passed over us, not knowing when a flight would turn out to be Jerries. Then this large formation passed over us heading northwest. Suddenly they peeled off and started to dive-bomb the landing barges.

Someone screamed over the radio, "Hell, they're Jerries!" So we opened up and headed for them. They were going pretty fast as they had gained speed in their dive.

We turned towards them and I got in three long bursts at about 90° deflection. I could see my tracers going right into the center of that mob of about fifty ships but I didn't see any appear to be damaged so I figure I didn't hit anything. Being fairly low on gas we returned to base. Logged 4 hours and 20 minutes. Logged 4 hours next day on escort to Sicily making my total flying time 47 hours and 55 minutes now.

Letter written June 21, 1943

Dear Dad & Mom,

I should be ashamed of myself, I know, for not writing sooner.... I'm just writing this to let you know I'm still okay. I hope you are the same.

The weather is still pretty hot here. I suppose the weather there *(in Pasadena, California)* is pretty hot, too. Don't know what else to write so I guess I'll just make this real short.

Your loving son, Donn

P.S. Could you possibly send me any caramels or butterscotch or walnuts or anything? Sure would appreciate it. Can't get it here.

Letter written July 15, 1943

Dear Dad and Mom,

I haven't … written for a week or more, I guess. It's so awfully, unbear-ably hot here every day now and the flies are so terrible. I'm plenty tired of Africa.

You ought to see my ship now. On one side of the gondola in big letters

is printed "Norma" in a kind of an arc like this — $NORM_A$ — and on the other side there is a skeleton in a white robe, sitting on a bomb with a scythe in his hand and a title, *"The Grim Reaper"* – looks pretty good, I think.

I flew 4 hours today and 4 hours yesterday and 2 hours the day before. I'm 1/3 finished now – 1/3 of my combat time is over with. Oh, I'll be the happiest guy in the whole world when I'm through, even if I don't get to come home. It'd be so wonderful not to have to sweat out the next day's mission.

I hope all of you are well. I'm okay as ever. I think about home more than you realize. Can you possibly send me anything? I'd like so much to have chocolate or butterscotch or walnuts. ANYTHING!

Your loving son, Donn

From Donn's Flight Diary - July 16, 1943

I've just been too lazy to write anything in this makeshift diary for the past month. Have been "jumped[33]" a few times since I wrote last, but the last seven missions have been dive-bombing[34] and strafing[35] missions over Sicily, covering the invasion. Haven't met any enemy fighters. I set a truck on fire yesterday all by my lonesome. It really burnt. Got a few shots in at a jeep over in Sicily this morning before the soldiers had a chance to get out. Got a few of 'em.

---

33 Being "jumped" is when an enemy ship suddenly attacks your ship in the air.
34 P-38's could carry small bombs and were sometimes sent on dive-bombing missions.
35 "Strafing" is dropping quickly down and shooting the ship's guns as rapidly as pos-sible into an enemy target on the ground. The ship then quickly heads for home – or the next target – depending on what the instructions were for that mission

Well, here's the new casualties to date as near as I can remember. Burke, Britz, Shaw, Conn, my buddy Nielson, Kurba, Thompson – who bailed out, and Braun – who bailed out.

Letter - July 25, 1943

Dear Dad & Mother,

It's hot here again today. About 118°F. There is a very slight breeze though, and that helps quite a bit.

I flew out to a field on the Cape Bon Peninsula the other day and I bought a couple of souvenirs from some enlisted men who had been in some battles. I got a German officer's Luger pistol and an Italian officer's Beretta automatic. They are beautiful guns. Very fine souvenirs, I think. I had to "pay through the nose" for them, though.

In case you are interested, I'm an Element Leader now. I've been leading the second element on my last 6 or 8 combat missions. You start out flying in 2nd position – right behind the Flight Leader. Then you move to 4th position – the "Tail-end Charlie." After that you move to 3rd position (Element Leader) in the formation and maybe later you become a Flight Leader.

Operations officer told me last night that I'll be a Flight Leader after a few more missions. Then there is only one more possible step – Squadron Leader.

I hope you are all well. I'm okay and <u>I am being careful</u>. I expect to be home in October[36] – <u>MAYBE</u>.

Lots of love,

Donn

---

36 Donn and Norma's first baby was due to be born in October

Letter dated August 2, 1943

Dear Folks,

I'm the hospital again. This is getting to be a habit. I've got malaria[37] and I'll be here for 15-day treatment. I am broken hearted. I'm sure that I would have been home in time to be present when my baby is born if it weren't for this. I imagine I'll be home by Christmas, anyway, though....

I'm much pleased every time I find that you have visited Norma. She thinks so awfully much of you folks, and she must be terribly lonely. Thanks for dropping in on her, Pop.

I hope you are all okay. I'm fine, in spite of the fact that I'm in the hospital. I've had no fever for 2 days now, even though I had a temperature of over 105° the first night.

Awfully glad to get your letters. Keep writing and after I get out of the hospital I've just got 18 more times to go out and come back[38] and it will be finis[39] for me. I'll then be homeward bound, I hope. Your loving son, Donn

Letter from Hospital dated August 10, 1943

Dear Mother and Dad,

I'm still in the hospital but I think I'll get out in about four days. I feel fine. I should have been let out days ago. But, "Oh, no!"

Thanks for the photos you sent to me and for the candy, too. It's almost impossible to get candy over here.

As to promotions, I was put in for First Lieutenant, not second, first, but it "bounced." The big-wig up at higher headquarters said no flight officers would be promoted as far as he knew.

---

37 Malaria reached its highest level in the North African theater in 1943, with over 32,000 servicemen contracting it that year. It is a mosquito-borne infectious disease that causes symptoms that typically include fever, tiredness, vomiting and headaches.
38 Fliers went home after successfully flying 50 missions
39 Finis means "the end"

Kind of awkward at times. Several times I've had a Captain flying my wing. Doesn't exactly make sense having a Captain whose sole job is to protect a Flight Officer's tail. Oh, well. I'll be happy to come home as a Flight Officer.

Your loving son,

Donn

Letter - August 19, 1943

Dear Mom and Dad,

I'm just writing to let you know that I got out of the hospital a few days ago. I feel okay except for being a little weak. I flew 4 hours yesterday. It felt good to get back into the air again.

By the time this letter reaches you, Norma should have received the French, Italian and English money[40] I sent her for souvenirs. I sent her some Franc notes, Lire (pronounced lira) notes, and an English 10 shilling note....

It's still very hot here, and the flies are the most annoying things I've ever put up with in my life.

It'll sure be good to get back home – when I do?? – and eat good food, out of plates instead of mess kits, and have milk, and even good water and out of a glass instead of a canteen. Gosh! I'll bet you could sell milk for 5 or 10 dollars a quart to every guy over here. I haven't had any milk since I left the States. I guess no one has. Ah, well – such is life. I'll quit for now.

Your loving son,

Donn

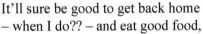

40 This is the money Donn sent to Norma

Letter dated August 21, 1943

Dear Mom & Dad,

Evidently I wasn't satisfied shooting down that ME-109 yesterday. I got a Macchi-202 today. A Macchi-202 is an Italian single engine fighter. I couldn't get a confirmation on the 202, but I know I got him. Had another tough scrap[41] today, but not quite as tough as the one yesterday.

Day off tomorrow, thank goodness. I don't think I could stand three scraps like these in 3 days. I'm really physically tired. A dogfight that lasts over 5 minutes is pretty long, but today's scrap was over 25 minutes.

We sent as many as 3 missions in a day over to Sicily. We sent two missions every day. That is just my squadron alone I'm talking about. Naturally the others were doing the same. We didn't have our usual briefing before these missions, as we had no definite target. These were just "targets of opportunity."

We made what might be called regular patrols over the enemy area. When we would spot a truck convoy we would go into echelon[42] and peel off for our dive-bomb run. In their excitement, time and again the enemy trucks would screech to a stop without bothering to have an interval between trucks. They would practically be bumper to bumper, which made hitting them much easier. The men  would often jump from the trucks before they had stopped. They would scatter into ditches and brush.

After dive-bombing, we would stay down and strafe the convoys from end to end, setting trucks on fire and trying to put them all out of commission. Then we'd head for home. Coming across the island we'd stay "on the deck" at about 50 feet maybe, and as the island is just one little hill after another, we would often come over a hill and surprise a jeep or truck and shoot it up before they could even come to a stop.

41 A "scrap" is a dogfight in the air with the planes diving, swooping, and zooming, each plane trying to shoot down enemy planes around them without getting shot themselves.
42 An "echelon" is a formation of planes in which each plane is positioned successively to the left or right of the rear unit to form an oblique or step-like line. Image used with permission from the 1st Fighter Group website.

I came over a little hill one day and there was a truckload of men tearing down a road. They didn't know I was there until I started shooting. Some of them I missed and they jumped from the speeding truck, but the main bunch didn't have much chance as I had all my guns blazing. They never did get out.

We also shot up a lot of trains. I enjoyed that. It was all really very "easy combat time." Another thrill I've had is seeing some of the things that I read about in school. I was on the first bombing raid in history on Rome. We escorted the bombers. I've seen Rome and Naples and good old Mt. Vesuvius with its smoking top, also the Vatican City and the Isle of Capri.

Incidentally, NOT ONE BOMB HIT IN OR NEAR THE VATICAN CITY. I know. I was there.

I guess that's all for now. I sure hope you are both in good health. Your loving son, Donn

Letter[43] - August 22, 1943

Dear Dad & Mom,

Well – we heard something on the radio tonight that sounded good to us. On the British news broadcast from London tonight the announcer mentioned that over a certain city, yesterday, a certain group of bombers' fighter escort engaged in one of the greatest air battles of the war over here. Well – boy – that was us.

Local Pilot Credited

The Associated Press reported that among the P38 Lightning pilots credited with victories in the Sicilian campaign was Flight Officer Donald D. Deisenroth of Sacramento.

That's the first time I've ever heard one of our battles mentioned over the radio. The scrap that the radio talked about tonight was the one I mentioned in yesterday's letter. It was plenty rough, but still not near as rough as the one the day before. I sure wish that I could tell you all about it. I will when I get home, though.

---

43 This newspaper clipping is about the battle Donn described in his Aug. 22nd letter.

I was leading a flight but it was split up by attacking enemy fighters. I went through the whole fight alone. I tried to join up with other ships of my squadron, but never could make it. I'd head for them and then I'd have to "break" into some attacking fighters.

My Intelligence Officer is putting me in for the D.F.C.[44] for helping some guys behind yesterday, but don't get excited as if it does go through it will be a long time, and it probably won't go through anyhow. At least don't say anything about it to anybody.

I hope you are all well. I'm okay.   Love, Donn
[45]

Later, the 1st Fighter Association wrote about some of the battles fought by Donn's unit — the 27th Squadron in the 1st Fighter Group.

On August 22nd the group's pilots began flying top-secret, low-level formation flights. Three squadrons launched maximum-effort missions each day and "everyone comes back looking like the cat that ate the canary." The group flew a well-rehearsed mission on August 25th. The target was the Foggia airfield complex in southern Italy. The 1st Fighter group launched sixty-five aircraft. After joining up with eighty-five more P-38s from other Fighter Groups, the 150-plane formation proceeded at extremely low altitude to the target area 530 miles from base. They hit eight airfields. The pilots swept across enemy fields strafing aircraft, gun positions, enemy troops and other military targets. The 1st Fighter Group won its first Distinguished Unit Citation for this mission.

Lightning Pilots Get Victory Credit

ALLIED HEADQUARTERS, North Africa, Aug. 22. (U.P.)—The following Lightning fighter pilots were credited with shooting down enemy planes Friday in the air battle over Aversa, Italy:

Flight Officer Donald Diezenroth of Sacramento, Cal., and Flight Officer Irvine M. Styer of Los Angeles.

While escorting Mitchells in a raid on Benevento the following Lightning pilot shot down enemy planes:

First Lt. Lawrence P. Liebers, Burbank, Cal.

---

44 D.F.C. stands for the Distinguished Flying Cross medal – apparently Donn didn't get it, as it isn't one of his medals.

45 Donn's last name — Deisenroth — was spelled incorrectly in this newspaper article.

[46]"Flight Officer Donald B Deisenroth of Pasadena shot down enemy planes last Friday in an air battle over Aversa, Italy, while piloting a P-38. Previously he had participated in the first Allied air raid on Rome, and he also played an important part in the air battles over Sicily. Flight Officer Irvine M. Sayer, Los Angeles, also shot down planes in last week's battle, according to reports.

Nazi Planes Shot Down Over Italy by Pasadenan

"Flight Officer Deisenroth had been out of an Army hospital only a few days after recovering from an attack of malaria before participating in last week's aerial battle. But for the malaria, Donald believes he would have been home when his baby was born...."

Donn's next major mission was on August 30th. The 1st Fighter Association said this about that mission:

The group launched a 44 plane formation to escort bomber groups to attack the Railroad Marshalling Yard at Aversa, Italy. As the American formation crossed the Italian coast, 75-100 enemy fighters attacked it.

The P-38s, outnumbered by at least two to one, met the defending fighters. During a forty-minute air battle, the group destroyed eight, probably destroyed three and damaged three more German aircraft, at a cost of thirteen missing P-38s.

The bomber formation completed its work without interference and returned to base without a loss. In 1946, the group received a second Distinguished Unit Citation for its performance on this mission.

---

46 In this account of the same battle by a different newspaper the bulk of the article repeated word for word what was in Donn's letter to his parents dated August 21st — about the Vatican City and his missions — so only the beginning of the article is quoted here.

Part Three – Missing In Action

Eight days after Donn wrote to his parents about hearing about that big battle on the radio, Norma received the following telegram:

THE SECRETARY OF WAR DESIRES ME TO EXPRESS HIS DEEP REGRET THAT YOUR HUSBAND FLIGHT OFFICER DONALD B. DEISENROTH HAS BEEN REPORTED MISSING IN ACTION SINCE THIRTY AUGUST IN THE NORTH AFRICAN AREA IF FURTHER DETAILS OR OTHER INFORMATION ARE RECEIVED YOU WILL BE PROMPTLY NOTIFIED

…THE ADJUTANT GENERAL

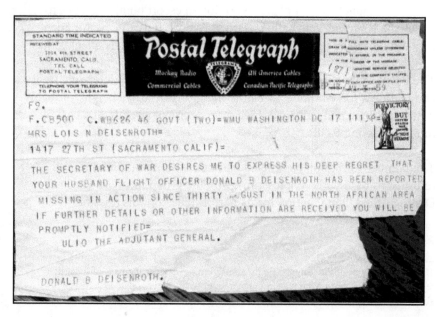

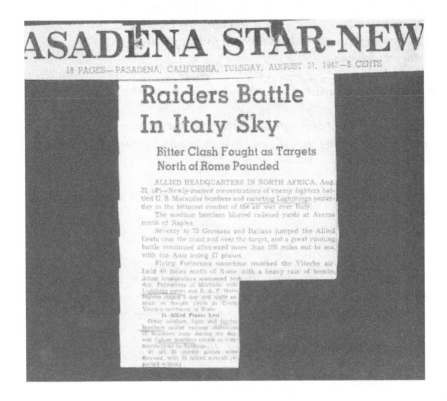

Raiders Battle In Italy Sky[47]

Bitter Clash Fought as Targets North of Rome Pounded
ALLIED HEADQUARTERS IN NORTH AFRICA. AUG. 31 A/P

Newly-massed concentrations of enemy fighters battled U.S. Marauder bombers and escorting Lightnings[48] yesterday in the bitterest combat of the air war over Italy. The medium bombers blasted railroad yards at Aversa north of Naples.

Seventy to 75 Germans and Italians jumped the Allied fleets near the coast and over the target, and a great running battle continued afterward more than 100 miles out to sea, with the Axis losing 17 planes.

---

47 Text from this newspaper article is quoted here
48 A P-38 fighter plane was also known as a P-38 Lightning

Flying Fortresses meantime smacked the Viterbo airfield 40 miles north of Rome with a heavy rain of bombs, Allied headquarters announced today. Formations of Mitchells with Lightning escort and R.A.F. Wellingtons staged a day and night assault on freight yards at Civita Vecchia northwest of Rome.

15 Allied Planes Lost[49]

Other medium, light and fighter bombers raided railway objectives in Southern Italy during the day, and fighter-bombers struck at communications in Sardinia.

In all, 21 enemy planes were downed, with 15 Allied aircraft reported missing.

A few weeks later, a letter from Donn dated August 28, 1943 was forwarded to Donn's father. This letter was received the end of September with the following note written on the top of the letter:

"9/18/43 Missing in Action since Aug. 30. War Dept."

Dear Mom & Dad,

It seems to be getting rougher and rougher every day now. I've been in a scrap just about every day now for over a week. I only have 11 more missions to go though, and I'm through. I hope I can get them in right away. I'd like to get them in in eleven days, but can't do that. I have over 150 hours combat time now, and I've been in a lot of scraps and I have one confirmed victory, two that I am certain of, and very probably more. I'll no doubt be able to tell you a few stories that won't be uninteresting when I come home. I hope you are all in good health.

As you probably know, Sicily was invaded from the southeast. Previous to the invasion, I had been over the island a number of times, both on dive-bombing as well as bomber escort missions, softening them up for the invasion. I did not act as air cover for our invading forces. Other units of our Air Force did that. At no time were we in action over area held by the Allied forces. As soon as the island was invaded, the enemy started hurrying his troops and armored divisions over the many roads of Sicily, towards the southeast, to reinforce his threatened troops there.

---

49 Donn's was one of the Allied planes lost that day

Our job was to do everything and anything in our power to slow up or stop the enemy's reinforcements. We dive-bombed tank and troop concentrations, convoys, road intersections, bridges, and railroad stations and yards. We strafed trains, troops, and convoys. But remember that you don't have to worry about me all the time. I'm not in fights every day. I don't even fly every day and I don't fly <u>all</u> day when I do fly.

I'm in a much better spot than an infantry officer, I think. At least my fighting is clean, and depends a certain amount on skill as well as luck. If I have any luck at all, I'll get my time in and come home with lots of experiences and stories to tell.

I'm awfully glad that you are all well. I am fine. I even get entertainment now and then. I saw a movie last night and enjoyed it, even tho' it was kind of corny.

It's been rather hot here lately. The wind is blowing rather strongly now, though. That makes it considerably cooler. Ah, yes – by the way — when you write to me and put N.A.S.A.F. on the envelope, it means North African Strategic Air Force. So when over the radio you hear something about the N.A.S.A.F. you'll know that's me, too.

Thanks again, both of you, for your letters. They help. If only I could be home when my baby is born I'd be happy. It's going to torture me. I won't know if Norma is okay for weeks.

I'll close now.   Lots of love, Donn.

Letter sent to Donn's father dated October 5, 1943 from Headquarter-First Fighter Group, Office of the Chaplain.

My Dear Friends:

Your letter of September 20th came yesterday telling me that you had received the official notice from the War Department relative to Donn. I would have written to you sooner about it but we are required by Army regulations not to divulge information relative to casualties until the official notice from the War Department has been received by the nearest of kin, lest the information given by others be mis-information. That has sometimes happened.

Of course, when the men came back that day without Donn, I was grieved. Of all the men in his Squadron I believe Donn seemed most interested in my work. He seldom if ever missed a *(church)* service if it was possible for him to attend. We had talked together a good bit, because, I suppose, his background and mine have had so many points in common.

I was in the hospital, myself, when the word came that Donn was missing, so I had not seen him for several days to talk with him. However, as quickly as I could, I looked up the men who were flying in the formation with him to find out just what did happen. No one seems to know.

The man who was flying next to him said that they were making a turn to the left, and Donn was there, leading the flight. Someone called over the radio that a formation of "Jerries" were coming in to attack, so they swung to the right, and when the turn was completed, Donn just wasn't there.[50]

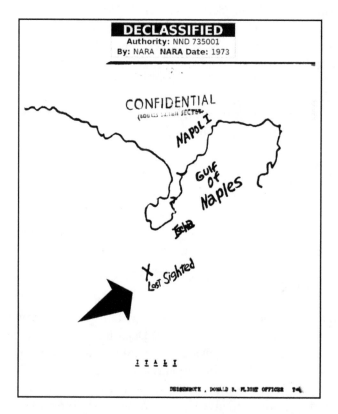

---

50 This official government document shows Donn's last known position before he was shot down, shown by the X on the map.

They did not think the Jerries were in close enough to get any hits at that moment, but it may be that for some reason Donn fell out of the formation and became a target for enemy planes later, for they go after a single plane in a big way. It is possible that his plane was hit in some vital part and he had to bail out.

At any rate, we are still hoping that he may turn up to be a prisoner of war (POW)[51] rather than actually gone. He apparently liked to fly, and when I talked with him he never seemed to be worried about flying in combat. And, he handled his plane well....

Relevant text from this article:

List Of Missing Includes Three Local Officers

Three Sacramento army officers are among the 574 United States soldiers announced as missing in action by the war department today.

They are:
First Lieutenant Robert B. Haley, husband of Barbara Haley of 1251 Cavanaugh Way, missing in the Middle Eastern war theater.

Second Lieutenant Donald P. Sabich, husband of Frances Sabich of 1217 P Street, missing in the Asiatic sector.

Flight Officer Donald B. Deisenroth, husband of Lois Deisenroth of 1417 Twenty Seventh Street, missing in the North African section.

The wives of each of the men were notified by the war department last month.

Other than giving the war theater in which they are missing, the war department announcement carried no details.

Lieutenant Haley, a navigator, was a former instructor at Mather Field. Mrs. Haley, who is attending the San Jose State Teachers College, is the daughter of Mr. and Mrs. Austin Brumley of 1251 Cavanaugh Way.

Second Lieutenant Sabich was a former highway patrolman. He figured in the news several months ago when he participated in the bombing raid on the Japanese base at Paramushiro.

Sabich, 29, received his commission last January and was sent to a fighting front in March. His wife is the former Frances Ravenscroft. The couple have a year old daughter, Mary. Zorka Sabich, a sister of the missing pilot, is an employe of the state personnel board. His parents, Mr. and Mrs. Stephen B. Sabich, live in Sacramento and New York City.

No information on Flight Officer Deisenroth is available. Neither he nor his wife is listed in the city or telephone directories.

Lt. Sabich

"Three Sacramento army officers are among the 574 soldiers announced as missing in action by the war department today. They are:

First Lieutenant Robert B. Haley, husband of Barbara Haley...missing in the Middle Eastern war theater.

Second Lieutenant Donald P. Sabich, husband of Frances Sabich...missing in the Asiatic sector.

Flight Officer Donald B. Deisenroth, husband of Lois (*Norma*) Deisenroth... missing in the North African section.

The wives of each of the men were notified by the war department last month...."

.

---

51 A Prisoner Of War was known as a POW

Text from newspaper article from Sept. 21, 1943:

Flight Officer Donald B. Deisenroth, who was credited with shooting down several enemy planes in air battles over Italy as well as during the battle of Sicily, has been missing in action in the Mediterranean war zone since Aug. 30, his parents, Mr. and Mrs. J. Bruce Deisenroth, disclosed last night. Notice to that effect had been received from the War Department.

. Sept. 21.

Flyer Missing in Action in Mediterranean

Donald Deisenroth Unreported Since Action on Aug. 30

Flight Officer Donald B. Deisenroth, who was credited with shooting down several enemy planes in air battles over Italy as well as during the battle of Sicily, has been missing in action in the Mediterranean war zone since Aug. 30, his parents, Mr. and Mrs. J. Bruce Deisenroth, disclosed last night. Notice to that effect had been received from the War Department.

The Pasadena air veteran, whose home is at 829 North Los Robles Avenue, was mentioned by his commanding officer for the Distinguished Flying Cross shortly before he was lost, Mr. Deisenroth reported last night. In a letter written Aug. 28, the flyer said that he was operating as a flight leader and that during the previous six days he had been in continual hard combat action.

Much of the action he had described in earlier letters concerned dive bomber attacks on troop concentrations, strafing of convoys, and escorting bombers on missions including the initial bombing of Rome.

D. B. DEISENROTH

The Pasadena air veteran, whose home is at 829 North Los Robles Avenue, was mentioned by his commanding officer for the Distinguished Flying Cross shortly before he was lost, Mr. Deisenroth reported last night.

In a letter written Aug. 28, the flyer said that he was operating as a flight leader and that during the previous six days he had been in continual hard combat action.

Much of the action he had described in earlier letters concerned dive bomber attacks on troop concentrations, strafing of convoys, and escorting bombers on missions, including the initial bombing of Rome.

Bruce Deisenroth, Donn's father, is sitting at his desk. He worked in the finance department of Pasadena City College.

Letter from Donn's father dated February 27, 1944, to the Adjutant General of the United States of America:

Dear Sir,

My son, Flight Officer Donald B. Deisenroth, was reported missing in action on August 30th, 1943, and no other official information has reached his wife, or us, his parents, since that date.

On November 24, 1943, a letter was written to his wife by one of his buddies who graduated and received his wings with him at Luke Field.

I quote Herbert Hickman's letter:

November 24, 1943

Mrs. Deisenroth,

Your letter of October 2nd was received yesterday and was glad to hear you were doing well. In your condition (pregnant) it must have been quite a blow to hear of Donn missing in action. You have my deepest sympathy.

HERBERT C. HICKMAN

By now you have probably heard from him, but in case you haven't he is safe and well. It is not possible to communicate with him but you may be able to through the Red Cross. I will see them and give them your address.

I am fine and have three missions to go. Will close with the best of everything to you and not to worry as Donn is safe.

Herb

Mrs. Deisenroth has written Lt. Hickman three or four letters asking for further information but has received no reply. He may have become a casualty or may have returned to the States and the letters have not reached him.

We are, naturally, very anxious to receive more word about our son and we thought you might be able to secure Lt. Hickman's present address so that we can find out what information he had when he wrote the letter.

We shall appreciate anything you are able to do in locating Lt. Hickman or securing further information about our son.

Yours very truly,

J.B. Deisenroth

This is Verla's house where Norma lived while she waited for Donn to come home from the war – and for their first baby to be born. Their healthy little girl, that Norma named Linda Lee, was born on October 20, 1943, while Donn was still (MIA) Missing In Action.

Verla

This article was in the Sacramento Bee. The text under the picture of Norma, Donn, and baby Linda Lee reads:

Flight Officer Donald B. Deisenroth, pictured in the inset, who has been missing in action in the North African theater of war since last August, never has seen his daughter, Linda Lee, shown with her mother, Mrs. Norma Deisenroth.

The Bee usually forwards prints of a service man's wife and baby to him, but in this instance the photos will go to Mrs. Deisenroth.

She last saw her husband March 3, 1942. Linda Lee was born October 20th.

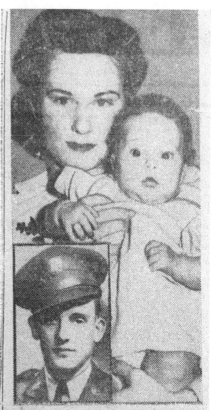

Norma's new baby was well-loved by everyone. Donn's mother, Adele, is on the left in this photo and Norma's mother, Lois, is on the right.

Flight Officer Donald B. Deisenroth, pictured in the inset, who has been missing in action in the North African theater of war since last August, never has seen his daughter, Linda Lee, shown with her mother, Mrs. Norma Deisenroth of 3732 Jeffrey Avenue. The Bee usually forwards prints of a service man's wife and baby to him, but in this instance the photos will go to Mrs. Deisenroth. She last saw her husband March 3, 1942. Linda Lee was born October 20th.   Bee Photo

Here is Donn's actual account (in his own handwriting) of how he was shot down:

"Got one engine knocked out after about 40 minutes, only lasted about 15 minutes more, then they shot my ship to ribbons. Bailed out on fire at 400 feet. Just barely made it. Almost drowned, couldn't get out of my chute. OK now, of course. I wasn't scratched."

Years later, Donn talked about being shot down in more detail.

"When I was shot down I ejected over the Mediterranean Ocean. My chute was pulling me under the water and I couldn't get it unbuckled. It was pulling me down.

When I realized I was drowning, something happened inside me and suddenly I was able to undo those buckles. I could have opened them with two fingers, they came apart so easily!

Once the chute was off, I popped back up to the surface and was able to swim to shore.

The Italians were waiting for me there and immediately took me captive.

I was not happy."

Ed Hyland

EDWARD J. HYLAND

On March 21, 1944, when Linda was 5 months old, Norma received a letter from another man who went to flight school with Donn. This letter gave additional details about Donn, giving her more hope that he would someday return home to her and to their beautiful little daughter.

Norma & Linda Lee

Text from Ed's letter:

Dear Mrs. Deisenroth,

I would like to give you some information about your husband which you may have already — I would have written much sooner except that I was led to believe that some one else had escaped and told everyone concerned with all the boys. However, yesterday I received a letter from the father of one of the boys in Prison Camp with me and he had heard nothing so I decided to rather give out old news rather than leave them with none.

To get to the point — Dutch (or Donn as you no doubt call him) is okay in every respect except one. He's still, to my knowledge, in enemy-held territory. We were all in prison together and all escaped to the hills together. However, another and myself left the rest on October 12, 1943, and walked down thru the lines and in due course were returned to the States. The same will happen to Donn when he gets thru the allied lines. He has, or rather had when I left, a long walk in front of him. It took us a month to make it and he may be hiding out with some friendly Italians until the Armies advance. At any rate, he is free as of my last knowledge (October 12, 1943) and uninjured and should be returning if he hasn't already.

The worst thing that can happen is recapture and internment in a German Prison Camp. And in my opinion, that won't happen. I think he'll make it. One thing he was really "sweating out" was becoming a father expected in October some time. He was pretty worried about you and how things were going. I'm very sorry I didn't write sooner Mrs. Deisenroth, but, as I said, I was under the impression you had been informed. For all I know, you may have been.

I trust you understand this is not official and shouldn't be given to the (*news*)papers or Red Cross or anyone like that. I sincerely hope you are in the best of health and also the baby and that you soon hear from Donn.

Sincerely,

Ed Hyland

The Italian prison mentioned in Ed's letter was Poggio Mirteto near the small village of San Valentino.

Map to show the location of Poggio Mirteto

Decades later, in the War Department Archives two records were disco-vered that contained information about the Italian prison camp and the escape that Donn participated in. Reports from Lt. Col. John Bright and 2nd Lt. Ed Hyland have been combined to give an accurate picture of what happened in that escape.

...Following interrogation <John Bright> was taken in a car to Poggio Mirteto where he found about forty other prisoners. They had been treated very badly and had practically no food for three days until they finally received some Red Cross parcels...

Bells and drunken soldiers which they heard on September 6th led them to believe that something important had happened. The next day they heard of the Armistice.[52]

On the 11th of September there was much confusion and everyone was advised to leave the camp.[53] They departed for the hills...leaving in groups of eight.[54]

They hid out in the hills, about six miles away and here they received food and news which was brought to them from the camp. They moved about the neighborhood for a week and six miles further on they came upon an Italian who spoke French and he led them to some woodcutters and charcoal men's shacks where they hid for ten days. There they heard that some of the helpers in the village had been shot by the Germans.

The party stayed in the hills where they were helped by an Italian family until their food became scarce. They were sustained also by Red Cross parcels brought from the camp.

Bright and Hyland left the group and started south (on their own) on the 12th of October. They reached the Allied lines on November 12, 1943, a month after they left the group.

Meantime, back at home, Norma spent a lot of time with her new baby. Her niece, Lois, continued to support her while Norma waited and *waited* for official confirmation that Donn was, in fact, not dead, but actually alive and well.

Norma and Lois

---

52 Italy had formally changed sides in the war, joining the Allied forces
53 The men in the Italian prison camp were afraid the Germans would arrive and take them prisoners (again) before the Allied forces reached them to free them
54 Donn left the camp in one of these groups

Part 4 - Prisoner of War

55

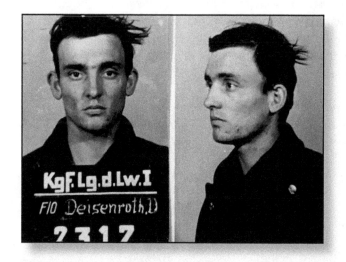

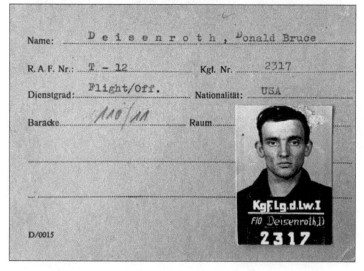

___

55 Donn's prisoner ID photos were taken shortly after being captured by Germans. The F/O before his name stands for Flight Officer.

Local Flight Officer Is German Prisoner

A war department announcement disclosed today Flight Officer Donald B. Deisenroth of Sacramento, who had been listed as missing in action, is a prisoner of war of the German Government. Flight Officer Deisenroth, the husband of Norma Deisenroth of 3732 Jeffrey Avenue and the father of Linda Lee Deisenroth, whom he never has seen, failed to return from a mission in the North African theater last August.

Donn's family finally received this letter a year after he wrote it.

I hope you are all OK. I'm feeling alright. Having a little dental work done each Tuesday, at present. My teeth are not in very good shape. Plenty of cavities and aches, etc. No toothbrush here and can't get one. At present life is just a bore. Nothing to do and the same monotonous routine each and every day.

It's very cold here. Strong winds and rain and snow. I'm glad I'm no longer out in it as I was in Italy. Many a time when I was trudging through the snow in a blizzard on top of some mountain, my thoughts turned to giving up. But always I could see you folks and my darling wife and baby in the distance so naturally I kept going. Sure glad it's over now, though. I wouldn't give a million bucks for what I went through, but I wouldn't do it again for anything in the world, much less a million bucks. Don't forget that this will all be just a bad dream someday. Write often and send lots of photos. With lots of love I remain, your Kriegsgefangene[56] son, Donn

---

56 A Kriegsgefangene (Kriegie for short) was what the prisoners of war were called in Donn's German prison camp

Mail sent from the German prison camp had to be written on a special form that was supplied to the prisoners by the guards. Their mail was censored before it was sent out. In this letter that Donn wrote, the date had been blacked out *<censored>*.

Outside   *Inside*

Letter from Donn' to his parents dated sometime in January, 1944. It was received by his parents on April 28, 1944.

Dear Mother & Father,

Awfully sorry I couldn't be with you for Christmas, but "Jerry" picked me up December 3rd about 20 kilometers from British lines. I almost made it. I'm in another transit camp awaiting removal to an Air Force camp. I'm well, so don't worry. Please write often and make the letters as long as possible. Send photos right away.

Your loving son, Donald B Deisenroth

Even though he wasn't receiving any mail from home, Donn continued to write to Norma and his parents on a regular basis.

Letter to Norma written by Donn on April 15, 1944, nearly 8 months after he was shot down.

Norma Darling, It has made me feel a whole lot better to be able to write to you again at last. I've missed you, Dear, more than words can tell. "Jerry" picked me up December 3, 1943, at about 10 AM, between Opi and Villetta Barrea. Opi was about 20 kilometers from the lines. At the time I was almost glad to be captured as I was nearly frozen, being in an awful blizzard with only one shoe and about 8 inches of snow.[57]

I am in southern Germany now in another transit camp, awaiting removal to an Air Force camp somewhere else in Germany. I'm in good health so do not worry about me. I can only hope that you and our baby are in good health. I've worried no end about you, Dear. Be sure to send photos as often as possible and make all your letters very long and number them. Don't leave out anything. Tell me everything that has happened. Tell my mother and dad, "Hello," for me. I hope they are all well. Tell your folks, "Hello," too. Please send photos, Darling. Letters and photos are all I can have now. I want a photo of your folks as well as mine.

With more than love I am ever yours,

Dutch.

---

57 Photo of the hills in Italy during the winter used via Dreamstime ift.tt/1Ng353X

Undated letter to his parents

I don't know just what to write. I'm naturally sorry about letting you down and becoming a POW, but I really didn't have much choice. As I told you before, it was a case of either bailing out or going down in flames — naturally I bailed out.

You'll probably be able to send me a clothing parcel once every 3 months. You can't send me any food, but you can send chocolate. If you can send me a clothing parcel make it about 6 pounds of clothes and 4 pounds of milk chocolate. Don't worry about my health. I'm OK physically. Write to me as often as you can, and be sure to send photographs.

I should be moved out of here within the next couple of weeks, to a permanent camp, where you can write to me. I'll be sent to an Air Force Officers camp and I understand the living facilities are good there. I guess I'd better close now as I'm running out of space.[58]

Letter from Donn dated February 1, 1944

Dear Mother & Dad,

I'm at a permanent camp for Air Force Officers now. I can send three letters and four cards each month and there is no limit on incoming mail, so PLEASE WRITE OFTEN. After all that's all I can have here — letters and photos.

I came through Berlin. I rode on the Berlin subway, quite a thrill, that. Another windy day today, but no snow here, thank goodness. I can't tell you where I am in Germany, but I think the Red Cross can tell you from my return address. We're living in barracks and have a stove[59] in each room.

My health is OK…. Tell everyone "hello" for me. I hope to be home in a year or less maybe.

Lots of love to you all, Your loving son,
Donn

---

58 Prisoners were only allowed one letter "form" at a time. When they ran out of room on the form, they had to end their letter.
59 Stoves like this one were the only source of heat for the Kriegies. Photo from Behind Barbed Wire.

If Donn had made it past the "lines" while he was an escapee in Italy he would have been in Allied territory and would then have been free to return to his base to continue fighting in the war. Donn complained bitterly after the war because the Italians had switched sides (from the Axis to the Allies) too late in the war for him – just two weeks after he was captured by the Italians.

This telegram was received by Norma on April 1, 1944 — 8 months and 1 day after Donn was shot down. It was the first official notice Norma had gotten telling her that Donn was still alive and was a prisoner of war in Germany.

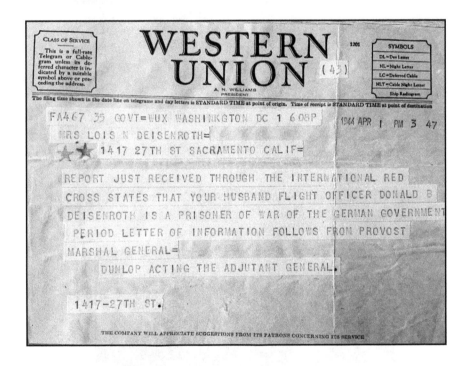

Letter to his parents from Donn dated March 10, 1944

Haven't written for some time I know. Haven't anything to write. Weather not too good now. Had a couple of good days last week tho! Hope you are all well. I'm OK as ever. Miss you all a lot. Hope I don't go "stir-nutty" before I get out of here. Not much to do unfortunately. Hoping to see you all in '45.

Lots of love from your son, Donn.

[60] These photos are of Barth, Germany, the guard tower in the prison camp and a room in the camp where up to 22 airmen slept and lived.

60 Photos from Behind Barbed Wire

Stalag Luft I POW prison camp had very strict rules[61] for the prisoners
to follow. The rules enforced by the Germans for the prison camp were
extensive and thorough.

Listed here are "some" of the 59 rules Donn had to follow while he was
a prisoner of war in Stalag Luft I prison camp. This prison camp had a
LOT of rules!

I.   <u>Camp Management</u>

    1. The language of the camp is German.

    2. Every German soldier, irrespective of his rank,
is superior to all P.O.W. when he is on duty. The
orders given by the German superiors must be
obeyed under all circumstances.

II.   <u>Camp Discipline</u>

    1. All P's.O.W.[62] are to salute the German officers
and military officials who are equal or superior in
rank.

    2. Roll Calls: As a rule there are two roll calls, one
in the morning, one in the evening.… P's.O.W.
are to stand on parade in proper clothing.

    3. Barracks (or blocks) are to be locked and shutters
closed at sundown.

III.   <u>The Following is Prohibited</u>

    1. To touch the warning wire and trespass upon the
area between the warning wire and barbed wire
fence.[63]

    2. Singing and playing of national anthems.

    3. Hoisting or hanging of national flags and em-
blems.

61 This partial list of the camp rules is from Behind Barbed Wire.
62 In the camp rules the Germans called the prisoners P's.O.W. for Prisoners Of War
63 A "warning wire" fence paralleled, at a five foot distance, the main enclosures.

4.To be in possession of any kind of arms or such-like instruments.

5.To wear a beard.

6.Unauthorized changing of quarters without previous permission.

7.To throw swill water and rubbish into the latrine pits.[64]

IV.   <u>Punishments</u> – In the following cases, P's.O.W. will be punished by disciplinary measures or by Court Martial.

1.For lack of respect towards German Officers.

2.For non-observance of instructions and orders that have been given, or for preventing the execution of same.

3.For hindering the German personnel in carrying out their duty.

4.For laying obstacles of any kind below the barrack floors. (Such obstacles were laid to hinder the work of German tunnel seekers.)

5.For insulting any personnel of the German Wehrmacht[65] or Authorities, verbally, by action, or in writing.

6.For attempting to bribe or incite German personnel to rebellion.

7.For willful damaging or destroying of equipments or articles belonging to the Reich.[66]

8.Willful wasting or spoiling of foodstuff of any kind.

9.Staying away from roll call without special permission.

---

64   A latrine pit was a deep hole in the ground which was used as a toilet.
65   Wehrmacht is the German word for Armed Forces
66   The Reich was Hitler's government

10.Improper behavior during roll call and during other specially appointed occasions (inappropriate clothing, smoking, reading, etc.).

11.For scribbling, damaging or tearing off German orders and notices.

V.   <u>Use of fire arms</u> – Fire arms will be used:

1.To ward off a bodily attack.

2.To enforce execution of a given order.

3.Against P's.O.W. who are met outside their quarters after lock-up.

4.Against P's.O.W. who are within the forbidden zone or who are attempting to enter it (touching the warning wire).

5.Against P's.O.W. who during an air raid warning are found outside their billets in the open air or standing in the block doorway or by the open windows.

6.Against P's.O.W. who are about to escape.

VI.   <u>Hygienic Precautionary Measure</u>

1.Living quarters and rooms are to be kept in a clean state. They must be thoroughly cleaned at regular periods.

2.Blankets must be repeatedly aired and dusted. Palliasses[67] must be shaken up.

3.Night latrines[68] must be emptied daily before the morning roll call.

---

67 Palliasses were straw mattresses
68 A night latrine was a bucket or pot used by the men in the barracks in place of the latrine pit because they were not allowed to go outside at night

VII. P.O.W. Mail

    1. Incoming mail will be distributed immediately after the receipt.

    2. Three letters and four postcards may monthly be written by every American or British Officer P.O.W.

    3. In urgent cases airmail letters and telegrams may be sent.

    4. Private parcels will be regularly issued after being examined by the Abwehr [69] Department.

VIII. Red Cross Parcels

    1. There will be a regular issue to the amount of a day's ration.

    2. Only so many cans will be given out as empty have been returned.

IX. Canteen

    1. The P.O.W. may run their own Canteen. [70]

Letter from Donn dated March 18, 1944

Hello, Folks, Hoping you are all well. I'm OK. The sun was out for a change today, but there was the usual cold wind. Played a little volleyball though. Nothing new of course! Confidentially I'm tired of prison life. Too much monotony. Think I'm getting claustrophobia. WOW! Lots of love, as ever, Your loving son, Donn

---

69   Abwehr was German Intelligence
70   A Canteen was a military store

At the prison camp, Stalag Luft I, in Barth, Germany, Donn was in North Compound I, Block 10, Room (or Cell) 11.

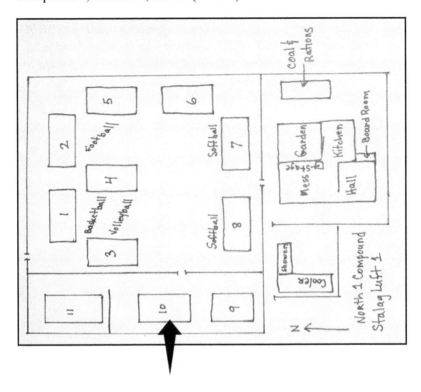

German guards entering Stalag Luft I, North Compound I[71].

---

71 Photo from Behind Barbed Wire

Donn was very grateful for *the Red Cross and the YMCA[72]. He often said how much they helped him during his prison days.*

The Red Cross sent many parcels of food to the prisoners and the YMCA issued each prisoner a War Log[73] (diary), which was treasured and used extensively by the prisoners. Many details of prison life were recorded in the men's War Logs, including Donn's.

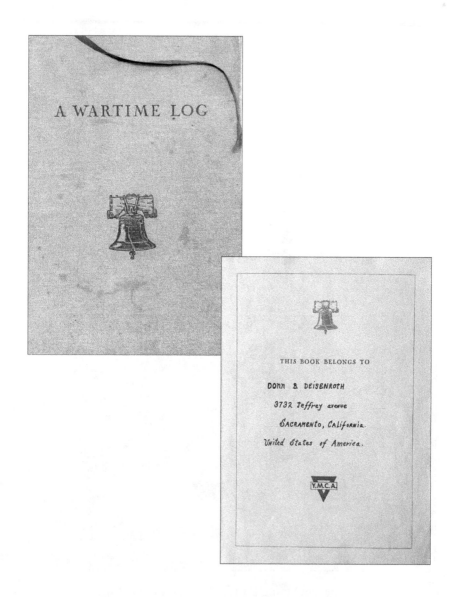

---

72   The YMCA is the Young Mens Christian Association
73   This is Donn's War Log

Donn's War Log[74] is incomplete in one significant way. All of the Personal pages (which he listed as beginning on page 120 in the Contents page of his Log) have been cut out of the book and were apparently destroyed at some point so that no one could ever read them.

CONTENTS

	Page
Songs and Poems	3 -
Addresses	35
New Concoctions	
DATES OF LETTERS AND PARCELS	100
PERSONAL.	120
MUSIC IN KRIEGGIELAND.	105

Donn carefully copied quite a few poems into his War Log., They obviously meant a lot to him. This "title page" he made in his War Log says:

KRIEGIE

Songs & Poems.

Some of these songs and poems are clean, most of them are NOT.

FOREWARNED IS FOREARMED.

READ AT YOUR OWN RISK!

---

74 The entries in Donn's War Log are in his own hand and were written in his book while he was in the prison camp. The pages pictured here have not been altered in any way except to turn them into black and white photos.

One of the poems from Donn's War Log:

[75]It is easy to be nice boys,
When everything's okay.
It is easy to be cheerful,
When you're having things your
way.

But can you hold your head up,
And take it on the chin,
When your heart is nearly
breaking
And you feel like giving in?

It was easy back in Africa
Amongst the friends and folks,
But now you miss the friendly
hand,
The joys, and songs, and jokes.

You've got to climb the hill boys,
It's no good turning back.
There's only one way home
And that is off the beaten track.

Remember you're American, and
that
When you reach the crest,
You'll see a valley, cool and
green,
AMERICA, at her best.

You know there is a saying
That "Sunshine follows rain."
And sure enough you'll realize
That joy will follow pain.

Let courage be your password,
Make fortitude your guide
And then, instead of grousing,
Just remember those who died.

* ANONYMOUS POEM
(found in cooler at Oulag Loft III)

It is easy to be nice boys,
when everything's O.K.
It is easy to be cheerful;
When your having things your way.
But can you hold your head up
And take it on the chin,
When your heart is nearly breaking
And you feel like giving in.

It was easy back in Africa
Amongst the friends and folks,
But now you miss the friendly hand,
The joys, and songs, and jokes

The road ahead is stormy,
And unless you're strong in mind
You'll find it isn't long before.
You're lagging far behind

You've got to climb the hill, boys.
It's no good turning back.
there's only one way home
And that is off the beaten track.
Remember you're American, and that
when you reach the crest,
You'll see a valley, cool and green,
AMERICA, at her best.

You know there is a saying
that "Sunshine follows Rain".
And sure enough you'll realize
that joy will follow pain
Let courage be your password
Make fortitude your guide
And then, instead of grousing
Just remember those who died.

75 Anonymous poem found in the "cooler" (solitary confinement cell) at Dulag Luft III

My Room-mates of BLOCK 10, ROOM 11.

2nd Lt. John M. Bender
711 State St.
St. Joseph, Mich.

F/o Robert A. Hoover
3904 Gallatin Rd.
Nashville, Tenn.

2nd Lt. Charles M. Allen
Corbitt Place.
Austin, Minn.

2nd Lt. Harold R. Madsen
McDonald, Kansas.

2nd Lt. Robert K. Belk
10031 Calvin St.
Wilkinsburg, Pa.

F/o John E. Monroe
45 N. Nice St.
Frackville, Pa.

2nd Lt. William N. Bitterman
503 Waco St.
Corpus Christi, Texas.

2nd Lt. James F. Lynn
4613 W. 49th St.
Kansas City, Kan.

2nd Lt. Carl R. Browning
2253 Lathrop.
Kansas City, Kansas.

2nd Lt. Edward S. Shumski
8801 - 91st Ave.
Woodhaven, N.J.

2nd Lt. Robert P. Bird
12 Stark Rd.
Worcester, Mass.

1st Lt. Bernard W. Walter
3016 - 9th St.
S.W. Canton, Ohio.

2nd Lt. Claude C. Edwards
143 Trammell St.
Marietta, Georgia.

2nd Lt. Arlo E. Warp
4301 W. North Ave.
Chicago, Ill.

1st. Lt. Lowell K. Hess
1802 Avenue "S"
Lubbock, Texas.

Here is a list of Donn's roommates just as he wrote them down in his log book.

He had a lot of roommates and by the end of the war there were 20 men (or more) living in each room.

Food was a serious business in the prison camp. There never seemed to be enough of it. Donn complained a lot about how much he missed foods he loved to eat. Allied airplanes were steadily bombing the German supply lines and the longer the war raged on, the more difficult it became for food to reach the prisoners.

Tucked into Donn's War Log was a ten-day menu of the foods the Germans actually fed the prisoners. They only got two meals a day, breakfast and dinner. This menu was typical of the food fed to them the entire 19 months Donn was in the prison camp.

[76]*Menu for week of January 13 – 22*

	BREAKFAST	DINNER
Saturday	Barley	Stew (150 M. Meat) or Fresh M. Boiled Spuds and Mashed Turnips
Sunday	Creamed Pate (40M) Prunes (20M)	Salmon Chowder (470) 10M Fried Spuds & Peas
Monday	Fried Bread Fried Spuds	Stew (150Meat) Boiled Spuds & Sauerkraut
Tuesday	Cold Pate (1/4 per man) Prunes (200)	Sardines (1/8 can per man) Fried Spuds Mashed Turnips
Wednesday	Fried Bread Fried Spuds	Salmon Chowder (470) 10M Mashed Spuds (10M) Sauerkraut
Thursday	Cold Pate (1/4 can per man) Prunes (200) (over)	Sardines (1 can per man) Fried Spuds & Mashed Turnips Choc. Pudding 290C;75Ch;75M;4M
Friday	Creamed Beef (all) 75C; 40M Fried Spuds	Stew (150Meat) Boiled Spuds and Sauerkraut
Saturday	Barley	Sardines (1 per man) Mashed Spuds (10M) Mashed Turnips
Sunday	Cold Pate (1 per man(Prunes (200)	Salmon Chowder (470) 10M Fried Spuds Sauerkraut
Monday	Fried Bread Fried Spuds	Stew (150Meat) Boiled Spuds Mashed Turnips

76 The foods most often served in this menu were: Barley, Stew, Boiled Spuds (potatoes), Mashed Turnips, Creamed and Cold Pate (ground meat paste in a can, often made from liver), Salmon Chowder, Fried Bread, Sauerkraut, Prunes and Mashed Spuds.

When Donn talked (*years later*) about the food they were fed in the camp, he said, "We ate bugs whenever we could get them because we were so hungry for protein. The 'stews' and other 'meat' meals were just flavored water. But I have to say, the German guards were really decent to us. They ate the same things we did and when the Allied forces cut off their supply lines, they were just as hungry as we were!"

German bread and frozen potatoes were brought into the camp by carts and trucks. Food was prepared by the prisoners.[77]

---

77 Photos from Behind Barbed Wire

38 ___ How I've DREAMED OF THESE THINGS!!!!!!

Foods that I'm going to eat a lot of when I get home!

1. Eggs, with ham, bacon or sausages.
2. Hot cakes, Buckwheat cakes with butter & Vermont made maple syrup.
3. "   "   "   " Eggs, sausage etc,
4. Spaghetti and meatballs with tomato sauce.
5. Chinese rice and noodles.
6. Steaks, roast beef, chicken etc. lots of meat.
7. Lots of pastry - cream eclairs, custard eclairs, cheesecake, Hot Cross Buns, Nut Bread, Ice-Box cookies, chocolate cake, Brownies, and pie with whipped cream & ice cream. Hot apple pie with cheese and ice cream. chocolate pie with whipped cream.
8. Lots of ice cream, milk shakes, sodas, and Sundaes with nuts.
9. Plenty of chocolate and lots of nuts. Also MALTESERS
10. cantalope with ice cream.
11. Tapioca pudding.
12. Lettuce and tomato salad.
13. Lots of good coffee. Plenty of hot chocolate with marshmallows, and gingersnaps.
14. Lots of whitebread toast with real butter and lots of peanut butter, Jam, and cheese, etc.
15. Frozen peas with butter and salt.
16. Plenty of whole milk.
17. Hot milk toast with Jam.
19. Mashed (I think) Potatoes creamed with eggs.

From Donn's War Log — in Donn's own handwriting:

The text from the previous page in Donn's War Log:

HOW I'VE DREAMED OF THESE THINGS!!!!!!
Foods that I'm going to eat a lot of when I get home!

1. Eggs
2. Hot cakes, buckwheat cakes with Vermont made maple syrup
3. Hot cakes, buckwheat cakes with syrup, eggs, sausage, etc.
4. Spaghetti and meatballs w/tomato sauce
5. Chinese rice and noodles
6. Steaks, roast beef, chicken, etc. Lots of meat
7. Lots of pastry – cream eclairs, custard eclairs, cheesecake, brownies and pie with whipped cream and ice cream. Hot apple pie w/cheese and ice cream. Chocolate pie w/whipped cream.
8. Lots of ice cream, milk shakes, sodas and sundaes with <u>nuts</u>.
9. Plenty of chocolate and lots of nuts. Also <u>MALTESERS</u>[78]
10. Cantaloupe with ice cream
11. Tapioca pudding
12. Lettuce and tomato salad
13. Lots of good coffee. Plenty of hot chocolate w/marshmallows and gingersnaps
14. Lots of white bread toast with real butter and lots of peanut butter, jam, and cheese, etc.
15. Frozen peas w/butter and salt
16. Plenty of whole milk
17. Hot milk toast with jam
18. Mashed (I think) potatoes creamed with eggs

In later years, Donn's daughter noted that the foods he dreamed of in his War Log (chocolate, ice cream, lots of meat, etc.) are the foods they ate the most of while she was growing up and the foods the Germans fed him (boiled spuds, sauerkraut, turnips, barley, etc.) are foods they NEVER ate at home.

Donn was also often heard to say, "The two worst things about being a POW was that there was absolutely nothing for us to do all day, and every day was the same. We were bored half to death. And towards the end of the war we were HUNGRY all of the time!"

---

78 A malted ball (candy) covered with milk chocolate

The Red Cross helped by sending packages of food to the men in the prison camp and the days when those parcels arrived were celebrated by all of the prisoners. On March 26, 1945, Donn helped to unpack 498 Red Cross parcels and he wrote in his log book a list of everything the packages contained, including two non-edible items — 2536 packages of cigarettes and 1193 small bars of soap. (Cigarettes were not only smoked by the prisoners, they were also extremely valuable to use when bribing the German guards.)

41

Red Cross Parcels arrived at our camp on March 26, 1945.
The following is an inventory of 498 parcels.

corned Beef	32	▇▇▇▇▇ 12 oz. cans.
Sugar	507	one-half lb. boxes.
Jam	564	six oz. cans.
Cheese	500	half-lb. cans.
Margerine	500	one lb. cans.
Peanut Butter	92	5 oz. or 8 oz. cans.
Coffee	494	2 oz. cans.
"D" Ration chocolate	698	4 oz. bars.
M+M's	199	packets
Soap	1193	small bars.
Milk	498	one pound cans.
Cocoa Bev.	98	8 oz. cans.
Soup Mix.	337	packets
Cereal	96½	8 oz. boxes.
Crackers	533	8 oz. boxes.
Pate	313	6 oz. cans.
Prunes	214	one lb. boxes.
Raisins	204	one lb. boxes.
Cigarettes	2536	packages.
SPAM	472	▇▇▇▇. 12 oz. cans.
"C" Rations	492	▇▇▇▇ 12 oz. cans.
Salmon	236	5 oz. cans.
Tuna	219	5 oz. cans.
Sardines	96	2¾ oz. cans.

Food in the United States wasn't as plentiful as it was before the war and rationing was a normal part of life for people at home in the States. But they weren't the only country who had rationing imposed upon them. The Germans were on rations, too. These are two German ration stamps that Donn managed to tuck into his War Log during his time in the prison camp.

The Germans treated the prisoners quite well, everything considered, but all the Kriegies could do was sit around and wait for the war to end or attempt to escape. This was something they could and did attempt at regular intervals during their confinement.

The construction of a tunnel was the means of escape most often tried. There were a lot of problems involved in attempting to tunnel out — even if circumstances were favorable— but at Stalag Luft I, the chances of successfully completing a tunnel could not be termed at all favorable.

Despite repeated searches by the Germans, Kriegies still managed to fashion digging tools and various devices that were rigged to provide adequate ventilation for the diggers. In addition, arrangements had to be made to dispose of tons of excavated earth; and all this needed to be accomplished while escaping detection by ever-watchful guards.

To the escape-minded Kriegie, stray bits of wire, tin cans and scraps of wood could be turned into hammers, shovels, sledges, lamps and what-not. A truly ingenious and efficient ventilation system could be (and often was) constructed out of an ordinary packing case, a number of tin cans, and some woolen strips cut from overcoats. The packing case would act as a bellows, the cans as an airline, and the wool strips as insulation. Altogether, over 140 tunnels were dug in Stalag Luft I, some over 300 feet in length.

After the war, Donn occasionally talked about an abortive escape attempt that he had made with his cellmates in the prison camp. All he ever said about it was, "We tried to tunnel out, but we didn't make it."

Years later Donn's daughter was able to locate the following excerpt from the memoirs of 1st Lt. Robert P. Bird, AAF 449th Bomb Group – one of Donn's cellmates in Stalag Luft I. Robert's memoir told about their escape attempt in great detail. It is reproduced here with permission from Robert's son, Sheldon.

Many unsuccessful tunnels were dug, including the one I participated in. We cut a trapdoor in the floor of our room and could drop to the sandy earth below. We crawled to the far side of the barracks next to a road and started our tunnel there. The objective was to dig under the barbed wire and the road and come up in some brush on the other side.

There was open country outside of the camp and the Baltic Sea was only about a mile away. It was hoped that if we could get out of the camp we might find a boat and make the crossing to Sweden. The soil in the camp was very sandy and the water table would not let us dig more than about eight feet deep. This was probably why there were no successful tunnels.

We had to reinforce our tunnel with wooden slats from our beds to pre-vent cave-ins. The slats were replaced with de-barbed wire from an aban-doned section of fence within our compound. It looked like the supply of boards would dictate the length of the tunnel, and it was questionable that it could be long enough to reach the target area.

Our room, which had started out with ten men, had grown, due to the efforts of the Luftwaffe[79], to sixteen, so we had plenty of tunnel workers. Light was furnished by "butter" lamps, made with pieces of suspender and oleo[80]. The air became so foul that we had to construct a ventilation system using cans for ducting buried in the tunnel floor and a bellows made from hinged boards and oil-impregnated sheets.

The problem of disposing of the excavated soil bothered us. We could spread the soil out under the barracks, but the peculiar color would give us away and if the space under the floor was decreased markedly the Germans would be alerted. We felt that the best place was in the attic of our barracks. It was a large space with ample room to accommodate all the sand we removed.

We started spreading the sand at one end of the barracks, gradually working our way back to our room which was in the center of the building. The sand was brought back to the trapdoor in the floor and then hoisted directly up through a matching trapdoor in the ceiling, thence to the far end of the building. Each night we would cover the entrance to the tunnel with boards and about a foot of sand so the Dobermans, German Shepherds and human "ferrets"[81] who roamed the camp at night could not discover it.

Great progress was made and the tunnel extended under the barbed wire and half way under the street. One night however, soon after lights out, the weight of the sand became too great for the barracks' structure and the ceiling caved in on the unsuspecting sleeping occupants in the end room. The loud noise of the collapse, which was accompanied by the very loud cursing of the men under the dislodged ceiling, alerted the German guards to the problem.

Whenever the possibility of a tunnel was discovered, the entire camp was turned out on parade until it had been completely investigated and all personnel accounted for. Needless to say, that particular night we stood on parade for several hours while the Jerries demolished our tunnel and made sure that no one was missing.

---

79 Luftwaffe was the official name of the German Air Force
80 Oleo was the brand name of a margarine
81 "Ferrets" were what the Kriegies called the nighttime German guards

Roll call[82] and physical drill in the camp was a daily occurrence. The men had to line up twice a day — at least — and always whenever the guards suspected an escape attempt.

Mail from home was an anxiously awaited event and it was a very happy day for the prisoners when there was mail for them. Mail was often severely delayed.

Letter dated May 5, 1944, from Norma to one of her aunts.

Dear Auntie,

You asked me to let you know next time I heard from Donn…. Well… I got 3 letters and a card the other day. He can't tell much news, but I'll quote anything that might interest you. The letters are mostly Love.

"I'm now at a permanent camp for Air Force Officers. I can send three letters and four cards each month. In my first clothing parcel I need one or possibly two pairs of pajamas, a blue turtleneck sweater, a razor and blades and shaving soap, two toothbrushes, a good pair of gloves, two pairs of shorts and uppers, and a billfold, and any milk chocolate that's possible.

---

82 Photo from Behind Barbed Wire

If you're wondering why I don't write much about the baby we probably have that's because I don't know what to write because I don't even know if it is[83], much less what it is.[84]

I'm OK. Had a couple of teeth filled yesterday. Feel better now. No toothache. All I can do now is wait for mail (with photos) from you and hope for the end of the war.

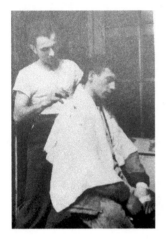

Your hubby turned barber[85] tonight. Another fellow cut my hair and I cut his. I'm sure he looks worse than I do, though.

I'd like you to give ten bucks a month to the Red Cross if you can. I've been meaning to tell you that since my first letter, but I keep forgetting. In my opinion the Red Cross is the most wonderful organization in the world. Many is the time since I went down that I've said, 'Thank God for the Red Cross.' " <The rest of this letter is missing>

Letter from Donn to his parents dated May 26, 1944

Dear Folks, Just a few lines to let you know that I'm okay. I hope you are all OK. I haven't received any mail yet unfortunately. I worry the mailman in my compound every day, until he swears that he'll bring me a letter the next, but as yet no luck. Sunshine for a change today, but also a cold wind. Weather is not too good here as a rule.

Lots of love as ever, Donn

---

83 Donn had no way of knowing (until letters finally reached him) if Norma's pregnancy had gone full term or whether (or not) she had successfully had their baby. She had previously had a miscarriage, so it was natural that he was concerned about her.
84 In those days there was no way to tell what sex a baby was until it was born.
85 Photo of a Kriegie cutting another prisoner's hair is from Behind Barbed Wire

This letter from Donn dated July 8, 1944, was received by his parents on October 5, 1944.

Dear Folks,

Needless to say I'm getting more or less disgusted watching mail arrive for fellows shot down in Jan. Feb. and even March. It's been a long <u>ten months</u> for me, without any word. If I only knew that Norma was all right it would help such a lot. I don't care at all about the baby. My only fervent prayer is that Norma is 100% OK. Naturally, I hope the baby is OK, but it means less than nothing to me compared with my darling wife. You can't possibly realize how perfect she was to and for me. During all these thoughtful months, believe it or not, I haven't yet found one place that she's failed me. She's such a wonder; faithful, thoughtful, loving, tolerant, and then so darn cute on top of all that. She's really a topper.[86]

I hope you all are in the best of health. I'm OK. Take good care of yourselves and "Squirt," for me. I'm getting low on space so I'll close for now. Hoping to get some mail soon. Keep your chins up because I should be home next year.

Your loving son, Donn B. Deisenroth

Letter from Donn dated August 5, 1944

Dear Folks, Thought I'd better write because it's been quite a while since I last wrote to you. Naturally, I've not received any word yet. I keep hoping as I've been hoping for the past 9 ½ months that nothing happened to Norma during childbirth[87]. It's such a dangerous thing and I've been worried so long now without knowing, that naturally I'm rather discouraged.

---

86 To Donn, a "topper" was a very special, perfect person
87 Medicine wasn't nearly as advanced in the 1940s as it is today and some women died in childbirth. The 9 ½ months that Donn mentioned was the time that had passed since their baby was due to be born — it had been nearly a year since he was shot down.

The weather here has been much better the last month. I've been out in the sun a lot. I've gotten a better tan than I've ever had in my life before. I hope you are all OK. I suppose Sis has married "Jeeps" by now. If so, I hope she'll be awfully happy....

In case it takes 5 months for this letter to reach you, here's wishing all of you a very merry Christmas and I HOPE I'LL BE THERE.

As ever, Your Loving "Kriegie" son, Donn

Letter from Donn dated August 11, 1944

Dear Folks, Just a few lines to let you know I'm OK. Weather has been much better lately.

I've got the best tan I've ever had. Beautiful day today, but maybe a little too hot. It's 10:00 pm and we're having a real thunderstorm. Three hours ago the sun was out. Weather changes rather rapidly here. No mail yet.

Lots of love, from your son, Donn

A letter from Donn dated August 20, 1944, was a repeat of his previous letter, including his frustration at still not receiving any mail from home.

From Donn's War Log:

The first word I received from home was a cigarette parcel, which I received on August 31, 1944, one year and one day after I was shot down. I still didn't know whether or not Norma was OK. Nor did I know whether or not I was a father.

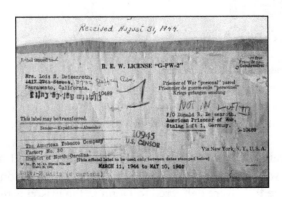

From Donn's War Log:

Then on September 26, 1944, I received my first letter. I decided to keep a record of any letters and parcels I might receive. The following is that record:

LETTERS

100

the first word I received from home, was a cigarette parcel, which I received on August 31, 1944. One year and one day after I was shot down. I still didn't know whether or not Norma was O.K. Nor did I know whether or not I was a father. then on September 26, 1944. I received my first letter. I decided to keep a record of any letters And parcels I might receive. The following is that record.

LETTERS			LETTERS		
SENDER	MAILED	RECEIVED	SENDER	MAILED	RECEIVED
DAD	JULY 1, 44	SEPT 26, 44	Norma	July 29, 44	Nov. 3, 44
Norma	July 5, 44	Oct. 5, 44	Norma	August 9, 44	Nov. 3, 44
Norma	July 7, 44	Oct. 5, 44	Norma	August 3, 44	Nov. 3, 44
DAD	July 9, 44	Oct. 5, 44	Norma	July 13, 44	Nov. 3, 44
SIS	June 8, 44	Oct. 5, 44	Norma	July 28, 44	Nov. 3, 44
Norma	May 23, 44	Oct. 6, 44	Norma	June 11, 44	Nov. 3, 44
Mom	July 8, 44	Oct. 6, 44	Norma	June 8, 44	Nov. 3, 44
DAD	June 17, 44	Oct. 6, 44	Norma	May 19, 44	Nov. 3, 44
Mom	June 2, 44	Oct. 11, 44	Linda Lee	August 25, 44	Nov. 3, 44
DAD	June 6, 44	Oct. 11, 44	Sis & C.L.	May 8, 44	Nov. 3, 44
DAD	May 27, 44	Oct. 11, 44	Mom	May 11, 44	Nov. 3, 44
Norma	June 24, 44	Oct. 11, 44	Dad	May 10, 44	Nov. 3, 44
Mom	June 18, 44	Oct. 11, 44	Carol Jeanne	APPROX. MAY 31, 44	Nov. 3, 44
DAD	June 10, 44	Oct. 11, 44	Norma	May 19, 44	Nov. 5, 44
Norma	May 28, 44	Oct. 12, 44	DAD	July 16, 44	Nov. 5, 44
Norma	June 3, 44	Oct. 12, 44	DAD	July 22, 44	Nov. 5, 44
Norma	July 14, 44	Oct. 21, 44	Norma	May 30, 44	Nov. 5, 44
DAD	May 3, 44	Oct. 21, 44	Norma	Aug 16, 44	Nov. 5, 44
Mom	May 2, 44	Oct. 21, 44	Sis & C.L.	June 24, 44	Nov. 5, 44
Norma	May 11, 44	Oct. 24, 44	Mom	July 24, 44	Nov. 5, 44
Norma	July 11, 44	Oct. 24, 44	Norma	July 24, 44	Nov. 5, 44
Mom	August 10, 44	Oct. 24, 44	DAD	June 29, 44	Nov. 5, 44
Norma	August 27, 44	Oct. 24, 44	Norma	May 11, 44	Nov. 6, 44
Mom	May 3, 44	Oct. 24, 44	Norma	May 3, 44	Nov. 6, 44
Norma	May 9, 44	Oct. 24, 44	Norma	June 19, 44	Nov. 6, 44
Norma	April 19, 44	Oct. 25, 44	Norma	RED CROSS COORDINATE	Nov. 6, 44
SIS	May 2, 44	Oct. 25, 44	Dad	July 3, 44	Nov. 6, 44
MRS. LATER	August 30, 44	Oct. 25, 44	Norma		Nov. 6, 44
Norma	May 21, 44	Oct. 25, 44	Mrs. PRENTISS	Aug 3, 44	Nov. 6, 44
DAD	August 16, 44	Oct. 25, 44	SIS	Aug. 11, 44	Nov. 6, 44
DAD	August 5, 44	Oct. 25, 44	Norma	Aug 8, 44	Nov. 6, 44
Norma	July 16, 44	Nov. 2, 44	Mom		Nov. 6, 44
Norma	August 1, 44	Nov. 2, 44	NORMA	May 3, 44	Nov. 18, 44
Mom & BECK	August 27, 44	Nov. 2, 44	NORMA	July 29, 44	Nov. 23, 44
Norma	May 1, 44	Nov. 2, 44	Norma	July 8, 44	Nov. 23, 44
Norma	April 24, 44	Nov. 3, 44	Norma		Nov. 23, 44
Norma	June 6, 44	Nov. 3, 44	DAD	APRIL 22, 44	Nov. 23, 44
Norma	July 14, 44	Nov. 3, 44	GRANDMA FALL	SEPT 28, 44	Nov. 23, 44
Norma	July 25, 44	Nov. 3, 44	REV. L.C. SHULTZ	SEPT 25, 44	Nov. 23, 44
Norma	July 27, 44	Nov. 3, 44	NORMA	MAY 14, 44	DEC. 5, 44
Norma	April 27, 44	Nov. 3, 44	NORMA	July 30, 44	DEC. 5, 44
Norma	July 31, 44	Nov. 3, 44	DAA	SEPT 23, 44	DEC. 6, 44

The letter Donn received on September 26th took three months to arrive. It was mailed on July 1st. In his log book he wrote down the date that each letter (and parcel) was mailed and the date that he received it.

Mail often came in "batches" and letters definitely did NOT arrive in the order in which they were mailed. Some letters took as long as seven months before they were delivered to Donn in the prison camp!

ender	LETTERS Mailed	Received	PARCELS CONTENTS	MAILED	101 RECEIVED
Norma	SEPT. 10, 1944.	DEC. 7, 1944.	32 PKGS. Luckies	3/11/44 to 5/10/44	August 3½,4
DAD	Oct. 14, 1944.	DEC. 7, 1944.			
NORMA	AUGUST 30, 1944.	DEC. 18, 1944.	Clothing	3/11/44 to 5/10/44	Oct. 6,44
NORMA	August 14, 1944.	DEC. 18, 1944.			
NORMA	SEPT. 5, 1944.	DEC. 18, 1944.	12 PKGS P.A.	3/11/44 To 5/10/44	Oct. 9, 44.
NORMA	August 24, 1944.	DEC. 18, 1944.			
NORMA	August 18, 1944.	DEC. 18, 1944.	6 cartons Luckies	5/11/44 To 7/10/44	Oct. 9, 44.
NORMA	August 16, 1944.	DEC. 18, 1944.			
NORMA	July 23, 1944.	DEC. 21, 1944.	Clothing	5/11/44 To 7/10/44	Oct. 25 44.
MOM	SEPT. 30, 1944.	DEC. 8, 1944.			
DAD	OCTOBER 14, 1944.	DEC. 8, 1944.	6 cartons Luckies	5/11/44 To 7/10/44	Nov. 8, 44
	CABLE-GRAM				
NORMA	Nov. — 1944.	FEB. 15, 1944	Food, Clothing	No Date	Nov. 29, 44.
NORMA	Nov. 22, 1944.	Feb. 15, 1945.		No Date	JAN. 22, 45.
NORMA	Nov. 23, 1944.	Feb. 15, 1945.	24 PKGS. P.A.	No Date	Feb. 4, 45.
DAD	Nov. 24, 1944.	Feb. 15, 1945.	6 cartons Luckies	No Date	MARCH 5,4
DAD	DEC. 2, 1944.	Feb. 15, 1945.		No Date	
SIS	SEPT. 11, 1944.	FEB. 15, 1945.	6 cartons Luckies		
NORMA	DEC. 2, 1944.	Feb. 16, 1945.		No Date	
NORMA	Oct. 26, 1944.	Feb. 21, 1945.			April 11, 45
NORMA	Oct. 27, 1944.	Feb. 21, 1945.	6 cartons Luckies	No Date	
NORMA	Oct. 23, 1944.	Feb. 21, 1945.			
NORMA	Nov. 27, 1944	Feb. 26, 1945.			
NORMA	DEC. 24, 1944.	March 6, 1945.			
NORMA	Jan. 2, 1945.	April 12, 1945.			
NORMA	Jan. 3, 1945.	April 12, 1945.			
NORMA	DEC. 26, 1945.	April 12, 1945.			
NORMA	DEC. 29, 1945.	April 12, 1945.			
NORMA	Jan 14, 1945.	April 13, 1945.			

Donn finally received official word that he was a father on December 8, 1944, from his father (through the government) — over a year after Linda was born on October 20, 1943. The text of that message reads:

Dear Sir,

We should be most grateful if you would kindly transmit to F/O Donald Bruce Deisenroth the following message received by cable dated 14.10.44 from the American Red Cross. "Norma and baby Linda fine everybody well many letters on way Father James Deisenroth." Thanking you for your help, we remain Yours Very Truly....

The middle of Donn's War Log came filled with empty photo pages — a "picture album" where prisoners could put photographs sent to them from home. Donn had many pages of photos in his book. Here are just a few of the photo pages that are in his War Log.

MY DARLING NORMA

Linda Lee at 6 Months April 1944.

Linda Lee at 8 Months.

Linda in her toy box.

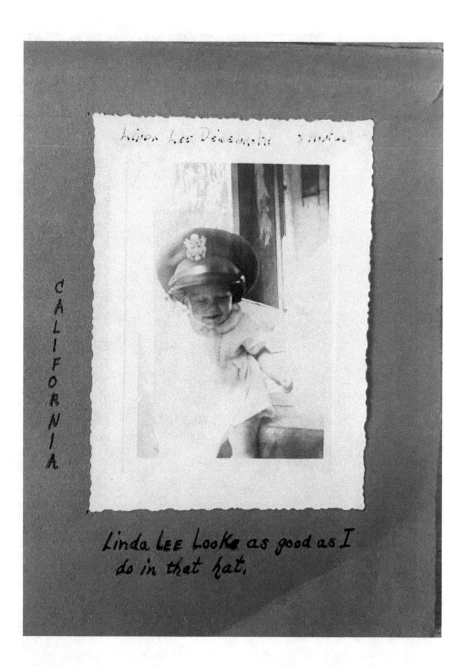

Linda Lee Looks as good as I
do in that hat.

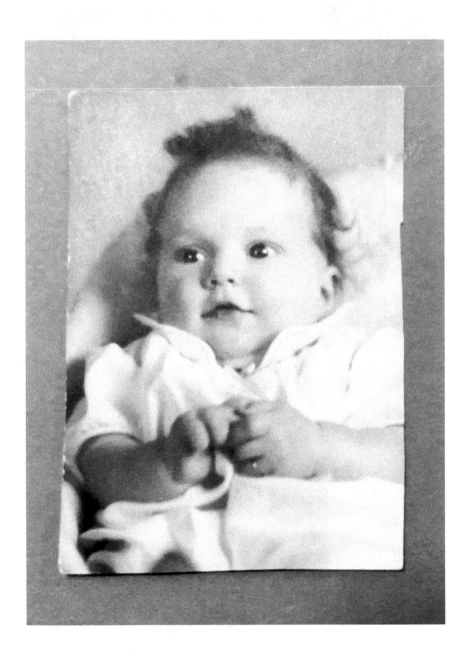

Verla with Linda Lee at 6 Mo.

Sacramento, California.

Linda
Lee
at
7 months.

June 1944.

Donn never got to see his daughter, Linda, during the entire first year of her life.

Miss Linda Lee Deisenroth
Age.-1 YEAR!

Mom, Dad, Sis, + ~~Sherry~~ Linda. May 1944.

PASADENA, CALIFORNIA.

Grandpa DEISENROTH with Linda LEE
at 6 months — May 1944.

Written under this photo of Donn's father wearing a woman's dress and hat while holding a doll is this caption:

Under the spreading chestnut tree the village idiot stands. OOPS!
That's my Pop!

UNDER THE SPREADING CHESTNUT TREE,
THE VILLAGE IDIOT STANDS. oops!
that's my Pop!

Donn's father obviously had a great sense of humor. That must have been where Donn got his because one of Donn's favorite things was playing jokes on people.

Norma

This letter written by Norma to her in-laws tells how complicated it was for Donn's family to send mail and packages to him while he was a POW. She wrote the entire letter in one paragraph, but it's broken down here to make it easier to read — and irrelevant parts have been deleted.

Dear Folks...

I received a whole mess of literature about writing, mailing packages etc. Every sixty days I'm supposed to receive two tobacco labels and one package label. My packages cannot exceed 11 pounds and has to be 18 inches in length or less, and it can't exceed 42 inches in length and girth combined.

The package should not be sealed and has to be wrapped so that it may be opened for postal inspection. These labels are sent only to me every 60 days....

I'm preparing his first package which must be sent before May 10. I'm sending comb, hairbrush, underwear, sox, etc. Toothbrush, powder, soap, safety razor (if I can locate one) and stuff like that. If you want to send any-thing in this parcel you better get it up here right away and I'll include it in the box...

Now, for letters to Donn. There is no limit to the number of letters that can be sent, however, the Red Cross advises that we write as few as possible. I'm going to write one a week. They also suggest that no one but the wife and mother or father write so there won't be too many letters going in and perhaps cause him to miss receiving any.

Loose snapshots and photographs may be sent. I enclosed a picture of Linda with me in the letter I wrote today. I'm going to put pictures of you and Pappy and you and my mother with Linda and a picture of my dad with linda in a wallet and include that with my next package. Letters should be type-written or printed so the German censors can translate faster and easier.

Packages may contain most anything except things made of metal. Oh, yes, the Red Cross also advises that we write short letters rather than long ones and no political news will pass the censor. Family and personal news is all the letters should contain...

Address the envelope like this:

> *Prisoner of War Mail*   *Postage Free*
>
> *<Address goes here>*

Then put that in another envelope and leave the outside envelope unsealed and put:

"Postmaster — Prisoner of War Mail" and no postage is required on prisoner of war mail.

Let me know if you want to send anything in this parcel I'm fixing now.

Loads of love and all that stuff,

Your DIL[88]

Norma

---

[88] DIL was short for Daughter-in-law

This is another poem copied from Donn's log book that meant a lot to him during his long, boring days of incarceration. It sums up perfectly how he felt about being in the prison camp.

Hitch in Hell

I'm sitting here and thinking
Of things I left behind,
And it's hard to put on paper
What's running through my mind.

I've flown assorted aircraft,
And covered miles of ground
A drearier place this side of Hell
Is waiting to be found.

But there's one consolation,
Sit closer while I tell.
When I die I'll go to heaven
For I've served my hitch in Hell.

June 1, 1944, Norma received a notice from the Military dated May 25, 1944, telling her that the government was sending a carton of Donn's personal effects to her. It cost her $3.61 to collect the box containing his belongings.

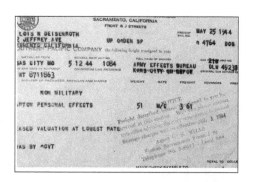

Prisoners were isolated from the rest of the world and the only news they got was what the Germans wanted them to hear and that was totally unacceptable to the Kriegies. They wanted to know the "real" news.

To accomplish this, parts to make a tiny radio set were smuggled into the camp by German guards in exchange for cigarettes. The radio was hidden in a barracks wall in the South Compound. News was written on toilet paper and was smuggled into Barracks 9, North Compound I in a hollow wrist watch where it was "printed" on two German typewriters.

Before lockup time at night, Kriegie guards were posted to alert the prisoners if a German guard was approaching and one copy of the POWWOW[89] "newspaper" was delivered to each barracks. The men read the news silently, quickly, in groups of three, then passed the paper on to the next group. The paper was immediately destroyed after all the men in that barracks had read the news.

---

89 This June 6, 1944, issue of the "POWWOW" is from the book, Behind Barbed Wire

Letter from Donn dated October 10, 1944

Dear Mom & Dad, Well I have received 8 letters now, 3 from Dad, 3 from Norma, 1 from Sis and 1 from Mom. I got a package from Norma October 6th with a picture of her and baby Linda at 6 ½ months. It's the only picture I have. How I treasure it. Mom dear, you asked me to tell you what happened to my one shoe? I don't understand. What shoe?

(Apparently Donn had forgotten — or blocked out — his earlier description about being half frozen when he was picked up by the Germans in a blizzard with only one shoe.)

Norma writes that I was Missing In Action for 8 months. You must have really thought I'd "bought it"[90] for keeps. It must have been horrible for my darling Norma, too, with a little baby. Norma is sure a topper. I've gotten 3 beautifully sweet letters from her. Well, take it easy, please don't forget to write to me. That's all I have here — letters. Don't worry about me. I'll be home one day. Keep an extra eye on that daughter of mine, too, I don't want her married to some soldier before I get home.

Lots of love, Donn

On one of the pages in Donn's War Log, he wrote down a list of foods Norma was learning to cook — dishes that he anticipated eating when he finally returned home.

"Some New Concoctions for Me at Home"

1. Banana Pudding (hot custard poured over bananas & vanilla wafers)
2. Apple Struddel
3. Peanut butter & banana sandwich, with lettuce
4. Condensed milk, also KLIM[91]
5. Creamed Spam and corned beef (powdered graham crackers) with croutons
6. Chocolate Pudding. (Graham crackers, cream, melted chocolate, sugar, nuts.)
7. Cheeseburger with ground up olives
8. Chocolate whipped cream (whipping cream and melted chocolate)
9. Tapioca pudding and milk and sugar
10. Sweet Potato Souffle
11. PEANUT BUTTER FUDGE

---

90 "Bought it" was slang for getting killed during the war
91 KLIM was a very dense milk powder that could be mixed with water to make "milk"

Letter from Lt. Don E. Falk to Norma (Donn's wife) received Oct. 2, 1944

Dear Mrs. Deisenroth,

I was in the same camp with your husband and was quite well acquainted with him. When I left camp in the latter part of July he was well and in good health.

A lot of the boys have received personal parcels from home and so their life is better by the mail and packages. The entertainment at camp is what the boys make and they have done a remarkable job.

The Red Cross and Y.M.C.A. have done outstanding work for us and all of the prisoners are terribly grateful to them. The religious activities at the camp are very good and I am sure you will be glad to hear that.

I hope <this letter> serves the purpose of having heard from someone who has seen him.

Most Sincerely Yours, Lt. Don E Falk

Letter to his parents from Donn dated November 3, 1944

Dear Dad & Mom,

Well my life here has been made much easier by your letters and Norma's photos of herself and Linda.

You can't imagine how proud I am of that little daughter of mine. What a kick I get out of the pictures of Linda — what a kid!

I want photos of both of you, too. Lots of them. If necessary, staple them to letter forms.

Sure wish I could get home soon — but now I guess I'm pessimistic as well as apathetic. I need cocoa and gingerbread mix, Aunt Jemima hot cake flour and soup mix and stuff like that. Lots of it. I don't think my last parcel weighed 4 lbs. WOW! I think Norma is allowed 11 or 15 lbs or something like that. A little milk chocolate is always good, too.

You've asked about August 30th. I got it in an awful tough scrap. Got one engine shot out and then in a few minutes my ship was really shot up bad. Finally bailed out on fire at about 400 ft. I was pretty lucky.

Better close now.

Lots of love, Your son, Donn

Meantime, while Donn was languishing in the prison camp, the Allied troops were making great progress in the war in Europe, which made the prisoners very happy except for one thing — the destruction of German supply lines hurt the German army, but it also adversely affected the Kriegies. The prisoners anticipated being released soon by the advancing Allied forces. On February 26, 1945, a "daily bulletin" posted for the Kriegies by the Office of Group Commander *(a prisoner in charge of his fellow inmates)* showed the seriousness of the prisoners' situation. Listed below are some of the items from that list.

DAILY BULLETIN:

1. Menu - No breakfasts until further notice. Dinner, German Soup (without potatoes).

2. Re Lights and Water - Water may be shut off at any time. It is recommended that a supply be kept on hand in your room. Lights will not be turned on at night for an indefinite period — possibly the duration *(of the war)*. Come on Joe.[92]

3. Red Cross food will run out Sunday. No more parcels are in camp and none are expected. Conserve what food you have, if any.

5. Coal rations will be cut another 20% effective immediately. The German authorities can guarantee no more coal. Come on Joe.

8. Personnel are requested to save cellophane from cigarette packages[93] for the prison hospital for making bandages.

10. Personnel who received bones from the Mess Hall for purposes of making soup will return same immediately. (For Re-Issue — they've already been cooked twice).

---

92 "Come on Joe" meant, Come on US Forces — come free us!
93 Every pack of cigarettes had a heavy, clear cellophane cover around it.

Norma received a letter dated February 28, 1945, telling her that an Air Medal, one silver and two bronze Oak-Leaf Clusters, representing seven additional awards had been awarded to Donn — "For meritorious achievement while participating in forty (40) sorties[94] against the enemy."

Donn was very proud of his medals and awards. He was heard once to say, "Those were hard-earned!"

---

94 The sorties mentioned here involved Donn flying on specific missions (and sometimes dropping bombs on targets) before returning to his base camp.

Every once in a while something special would take place in the prison camp — like on April 3, 1945 — the day Max Schmeling visited Stalag Luft I.

Donn was an avid boxing fan and when he found out the heavy-weight boxing champion of the world was visiting their prison camp, he ran as fast as he could to his cell and grabbed his war log so he could get Max's signature.

141

Signature of

Max Schmeling

at

Stalag luft I

Barth, Germany.

April 3, 1945.

Donn stood in a long line, but it was worth it. He was extremely happy to have Max Schmeling's signature.

LIBERATION!

The Allied forces kept pushing back the German army and on May 1, 1945, Russians arrived at Stalag Luft I in Barth, Germany, releasing over 9000 imprisoned men from the Germans. The Kriegies went mad with joy!

On May 8th, the Allies accepted Germany's unconditional surrender, formally ending the war in Europe. Shortly afterwards, the injured and

British prisoners were flown out of the camp and then on May 13th and 14th , the remaining prisoners were loaded into B-17s and were flown out of Germany and then later into London, England. Donn was one of those prisoners.

The North Compound[95] was very empty after all the prisoners were gone.

---

95 North compound photo from Behind Barbed Wire

But Germany's surrender didn't end the war with Japan, which continued to rage on, unchecked. Then, on Aug 6, 1945, the United States dropped an atomic bomb[96] on the Japanese city of Hiroshima. It was followed three days later by a second atomic bomb which also destroyed the city of Nagasaki. Hundreds of thousands of people were injured and killed in those two attacks.

On September 2, 1945, U.S. General Douglas MacArthur accepted Japan's unconditional surrender, ending the fighting.

WWII WAS OFFICIALLY OVER!

Once Donn was back under the control of the United States, he was allowed to write 15 words to Norma. His message had to be printed, in block letters. It read:

NORMA DARLING EXPECT ARRIVE LATE JUNE HOPE ALL WELL MISS MY PRECIOUS WIFE TERRIBLY LOVE – DONN B. DEISENROTH

A telegram was also sent to Norma from the Secretary of War, informing her that Donn had been returned to U.S. military control.

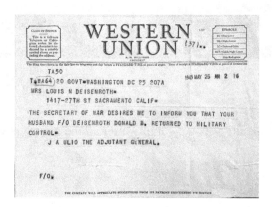

---

96 The first and only nuclear bombs to ever be used in war

Their last name, Deisenroth, was misspelled in this newspaper article.

Flier En Route Home

Mrs. Norma Edeisenroth of 3832 Jeffrey Avenue has received a letter from her husband, Flight Officer Donald B. Edeisenroth, stating he has been released and is en route home.

He had been a prisoner of war for about a year and a half. He was a P38 fighter pilot and wears the air medal with one silver and two bronze oak leaf clusters.

He will see his daughter, Linda, 1½, for the first time.

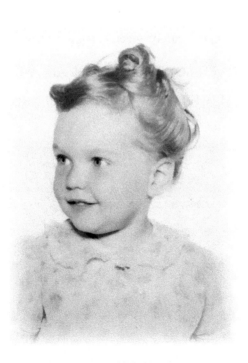

Linda Lee

After he returned home, Donn was awarded membership in "The Caterpillar Club." He received a one-inch long real gold caterpillar pin[97] with miniature ruby eyes with his membership card. It's a very tiny pin!

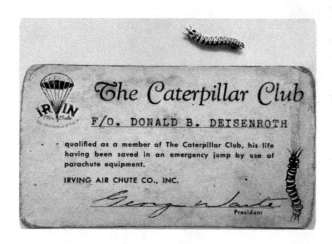

The card says: *F/O Donald B. Deisenroth qualified as a member of the Caterpillar Club, his life having been saved in an emergency jump by use of parachute equipment.*

This telegram was an extremely welcome sight to Norma. It reads:

DARLING ARRIVED LONDON OK HOPE ALL WELL REPLY

EXPOW DET ... MUCH LOVE =   DONN DEISENROTH

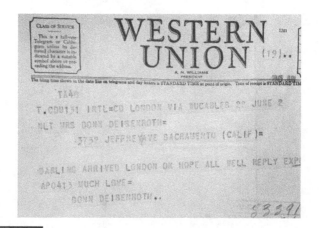

97 The gold pin is shown here with his Caterpillar Club card, which is about the size of a credit card.

Part Five - After the War

Donn was very skinny for quite awhile after he got home. He and Norma were so happy to be back together again and he was thrilled to finally meet his beautiful little daughter! (Linda, however, was not quite so happy to have to share her mother with this "strange man.")

Their second child was born nine months after he returned home.

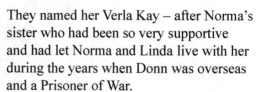

They named her Verla Kay – after Norma's sister who had been so very supportive and had let Norma and Linda live with her during the years when Donn was overseas and a Prisoner of War.

After he returned to the States, jobs weren't easy to get. Many men who had fought in the war were also looking for work. To help returning soldiers, President Franklin D. Roosevelt signed a Servicemen's Readjustment Act, known as the GI Bill. Among other things, the GI Bill authorized unemployment compensation of $20 per week for a maximum of 52 weeks and offered job placement aid and education and training for returning vets.

In 1947, Donn studied to be a fireman. It wasn't what he really wanted to do, but it was a job he could do while he was in the Army Air Force Reserves. When he took his fireman's test in Bakersfield, his score was 93.69 — it was the third highest score of everyone testing with him.

CITY OF BERKELEY
DEPARTMENT OF PERSONNEL AND RESEARCH

NOTICE OF TEST RESULTS

(X) YOU WERE SUCCESSFUL IN THE TESTS FOR THE POSITION, THE TITLE OF WHICH IS ENTERED ON THE REVERSE SIDE OF THIS CARD.

TEST SCORE ✶✶✶✶✶ 93.69

Your Position on ✶✶✶✶✶ List 3

( ) YOU WERE UNSUCCESSFUL IN THE TESTS FOR THIS POSITION FOR THE REASONS INDICATED BELOW—

☐ Your rating in the written tests was below the required percentage.
☐ Your rating on Education, Experience and Personal Qualifications was below the required percentage.
☐ Your rating was less than..............the required percentage in..........................
☐ Your rating in the Demonstration Test was below the required percentage.
☐ You failed to appear for the Demonstration Test.
☐ You failed to appear for Appraisal of Education, Experience and Personal Qualifications.

☐

SIX WORLD WAR II VETERANS NAMED TO BERKELEY FIRE DEPARTMENT

BERKELEY, Nov. 20.—Six World War II veterans have been appointed to the Berkeley Fire Department as hosemen as a result of competitive examinations recently conducted to set up an eligibility list to fill vacancies. Two of the appointees, Robert F. Hartkop, 27, 1749 Sacramento Street, and John E. Warok, 27, 1716 University Avenue, both Navy veterans, have been serving as provisional hose-

Other appointees are: George W. Deatherage, 26, 2532 Ridge Road, former Navy chief petty officer; Donald B. Deisenroth, 25, 155 South 12th Street, Richmond, former Air Force lieutenant; Howard E. Nichelman, 25, 1030 Ventura Avenue, Albany, former ensign in Maritime Service, and Jackson H. Boyd Jr., 23, Gilroy, a former Marine Corps Corporal. Chief William Meinheit announced that all appointments would be on a one-year proba-

Donn worried a lot about his family's future. His girls were growing fast and he wasn't really happy unless he was flying. Fighting fires was not what he wanted to do for the rest of his life.

Donn in his firefighter's suit and Verla Kay and Linda Lee

Then, in 1950, Donn was recalled to active service in the Air Force and was relocated to Norton Air Force Base in San Bernadino, CA, where he got to fly again. He flew F-80 Shooting Stars — the first jet fighter used operationally by the Air Force.

LIEUT. DONALD B. DEISEN-ROTH, 173 Santa Clara Avenue, has been recalled to active duty. He is a jet fighter pilot flying F-80 Shooting Stars with the 196th Fighter Squadron at Norton Air Base, San Bernardino. Lieut. Deisenroth will move with the unit to its new location at George AFB, Victorville. He is a graduate of Technical High School. He and his wife, Lois, have two children, Linda Lee, 7, and Verla Kay, 4.

Linda Lee, Grandpa Bruce (Donn's father) and Verla Kay

While his family was living in southern California, they were able to spend a lot of quality time with Donn's parents.

But Donn wasn't really happy flying jets. He said, "They aren't fun to fly like planes that have propellers," so he wasn't unhappy when he was transferred once again in 1951, to Chanute Air Force Base in Illinois.

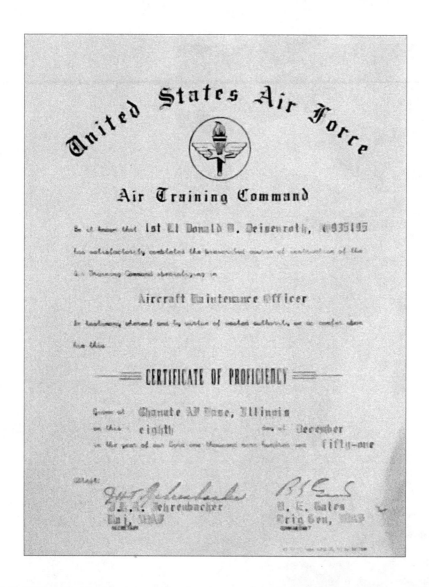

When he got there, he trained to be an aircraft maintenance officer and he also trained pilots. There was a lot of desk work involved. Donn would have preferred to have been flying most of the time, instead of sitting in a corner doing paperwork and answering phones.

Donn is at the corner desk, on the far right, talking on the phone.

While they lived in Illinois, Norma helped Linda and Verla Kay make a snow dog in their yard.

The girls used a metal garbage can lid as a sled and Norma spent many hours taming a squirrel to scamper down from the trees and eat nuts from her hand.

One memorable day, the family woke up to a loud noise.

When they walked into the kitchen, Norma and Donn were aghast when they saw that the old stove opening to the chimney (which currently serviced the boiler/heating system from the basement) had blown off a tin plate on the wall which had covered the hole and there was about a half of an inch of soot covering everything in the kitchen!

Soot was on the floors, in the cupboards, and it coated all the chairs and even went up and over the butter in the butter dish on the table.

The girls couldn't understand why their mother was crying.

To them it looked so FUNNY!

Donn's next transfer in 1952, was back to Luke Airfield in Arizona, where he and Norma had their third child — a boy they named Donn Michael.

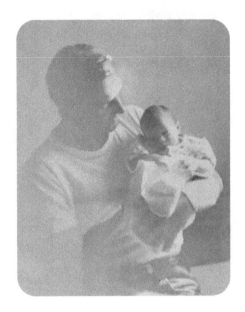

Donn was thrilled to have a son. Mike completed their family perfectly.

They called Linda "Windy," and Verla Kay was "Stormy" or "Yakkety-Yak" — because Verla's eyes flashed like storm clouds when she was angry and it was nearly impossible to get her to stop talking when she was awake.

Verla Kay vividly remembers a day when she was made to sit with tape across her mouth for several hours.[98] She mumbled and talked right through the tape the entire time.

She said later she had things she just HAD to say, and no piece of tape across her mouth was going to stop her!

---

98 Many child raising practices were acceptable and considered normal in those days that today would not be allowed at all.

Donn called Mike "Speedy Gonzales," because he was such a little live-wire.

Mike was a real character — just like his father— even when he was still a toddler.

For about a year, Mike was almost never seen without his favorite (ragged and misshapen) hat. He would only take it off when he was sleeping.

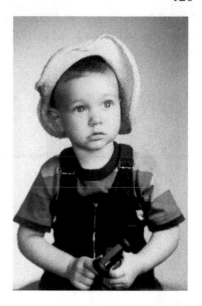

All this time Donn's family was growing and things were good for them, but what he really wanted to do was fly airplanes every day, so in 1953, when he got a job offer from Atwood Crop Dusters, he jumped at the chance.

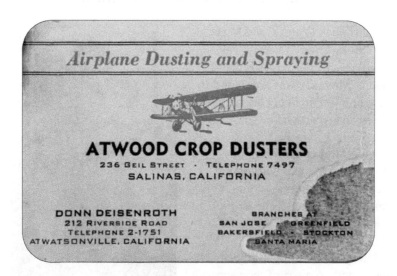

Donn immediately moved his family to Watsonville, California, where he flew crop dusters — spraying and dusting fields of strawberries, lettuce, apple orchards and many other crops.

His day began at the break of dawn because there was less wind early in the morning and he had to get the fields dusted when it wasn't windy, or the pesticides wouldn't land in the field he was dusting.

That happened one day when dust blew over onto a huge field of daisies that were about to be picked and shipped to florists.

The daisy farmer said the flowers were no longer fit to sell and he made Donn pay for the entire crop of flowers.

Donn was so angry, he drove out into the field and completely filled his entire pickup truck with daisies. They were heaped as high as he could get them in the truck.

He said, "If I have to pay for those #@&!$* flowers, I'm going to at least enjoy them!"

He brought them home, filled every room of his house with them and gave the rest of the daisies to everyone he knew — and he knew a LOT of people in town.

But the military wasn't through with Donn quite yet. The US and the Soviet Union had had an on-going political rivalry since the end of WWII — Communism vs Capitalism. In June of 1954, the CIA (US Central Intelligence Agency) got involved in a covert operation that deposed the President of Guatemala, who seemed to be leaning towards Communism.

Donn was one of the pilots sent there to help with this operation. His job was to fly reconnaissance planes and take aerial photographs of the topography and the locations of any troops or equipment.

Donn wrote on the back of this photograph: *This is me at the wheel on take-off. Wheels are going up, as you can see. Guatemala Airport.*

His family was planning to join him, but by the time they had gotten their necessary inoculations, the President of Guatemala had been deposed, and Donn was being sent home. Verla Kay remembers how unhappy she was that she had to have "all those shots for nothing!"

As soon as he returned home, he resumed his normal crop dusting duties. Because he only flew in the mornings when there was less wind, and he got his paperwork done quickly in the afternoons, Donn had a good amount of leisure time for himself, which he thoroughly enjoyed.

He did yard work around the house, planted a vegetable garden, played the clarinet and a recorder (neither one very well), and loved relaxing in a hammock after his day's work was done.

Some afternoons he would have to go to a local supplier to buy needed sacks of pesticides to use when he was dusting crops. If his children were around, he often took them with him and let them climb around and play on the sacks of pesticides. But there was one area in the warehouse where he would NOT let them play.

"Stay away from those sacks!" he would caution. "They aren't safe to climb on!"

Those were stacks of DDT — an extremely potent and dangerous pesticide. Following World War II, DDT was promoted and widely used as a highly effective solution to Malaria, Typhoid and pest problems, both in the fields and around homes.

But DDT was banned from use in 1970, by the Secretary of the Interior, because it was found to be extremely dangerous to both the environment and to human health.

Today it is believed that girls exposed to DDT before puberty were five times more likely to develop breast cancer in middle age.

It also is thought to have caused a severe decline in the population of bald eagles while it was in common use, because it apparently caused their egg shells to become extremely fragile.

Residue from DDT[99] was still being found in the ground 40 years after it had been banned!

Just about everyone in town knew and loved Donn. He and Norma were very active in the community. They were members of the Elks Lodge and Donn was active in the Masons.

They held lots of parties on a regular basis, often with as many as 50 people at a time in their home. They ate, drank and smoked[100] a lot. They played cards and "party" games and Norma and Donn always had as much fun as their guests.

Some of their parties were very loud with laughter, especially one day when they were playing "spoons" (a card game where there is one less spoon than people and the object is to not be the person left without a spoon).

When all of the adults dove into the middle of the kitchen table to try to get one of the spoons, a table leg broke off and everyone fell onto the floor in a big heap on top of the collapsed table.

---

99 Donn's crop duster being loaded with sacks of pesticides — some of which were DDT.
100 Smoking was considered "cool" in those days because no one knew how bad it was for their health.

But that didn't stop the game. The players kept rolling all over the floor, fighting for that last spoon! There was much laughter in spite of the demolished table.

Norma and Donn at one of their parties — on New Year's Eve

Donn was an exceptionally good crop duster pilot and people would marvel at his high, tight turns and the way he swooped straight down to get into position to dust the fields.

When he saw people on the ground, he would wave out of the plane — or, more often — he would "wave his wings" (dip the plane wings up and down, alternately) at the people down below. He loved to make people happy.

Donn's quirky sense of humor was rarely absent and occasionally he would hang out of the side of his plane, so it looked like he had passed out and no one was flying it — just to give people a thrill! He was very beloved by many people in the community.

Donn was honorably discharged from the Army on October 26, 1956. He was no longer at the beck and call of the military and didn't have to worry about being recalled to active duty or of being relocated to a new place with his family.

It was just four years later, September 7, 1960, and Donn had just finished training a new crop duster pilot in a Stearman trainer crop duster (ironically, the exact same kind of plane in which he first learned to fly). Donn got back into the Stearman (alone) to return the plane to a neighboring town when "something" happened. The plane started to take off, abruptly flipped upside down and crashed onto the runway, exploding in a giant ball of flames.[101]

Burned wreckage of cropduster trainer still contains body of Deisenroth. (Story above)

---

101 The caption under this newspaper photograph reads: "Burned wreckage of cropduster trainer still contains body of Deisenroth."

The medical examiner said Donn was dead on impact, but both he and the plane were so badly incinerated that no one will ever know whether it was a medical problem, pilot error, or a mechanical failure in the plane that caused the crash. Donn was 38 years old at the time of his death.

These are two of the last pictures taken of Donn and Norma before his death. They had just gotten dressed to go out that evening.

Donn (age 38)

Norma

It seems very fitting to end Donn's story with a special poem, which meant so much to him that he laboriously wrote it down by hand while in the German prison camp. It was one of his favorite poems and he treasured it greatly. There have been many copies of this poem published through the years. It has been copied here exactly as Donn wrote it. It is the ideal eulogy for him as it sums up his life perfectly.

The poem is:

"High Flight"
by Pilot Officer John Gillespie Magee[102]

I have slipped the surly bonds of earth
And danced the skies on laughter-silvered wings.
Sunward I've climbed and joined the tumbling mirth
Of sunsplit clouds – and done a hundred things
You have not dreamed of. Wheeled and soared and swung
High in the sunlit silence. Hovering there
I've chased the shouting wind along and flung
My eager craft through fearless halls of air.
 Up — — up the long delirious burning blue
I've topped the windswept heights with easy grace,
Where never lark — or ever eagle — flew.
And with silent lifting spirit I have trod
The high untrespassed sanctity of space —
Put out my hand,
And touched the face of God.

[103]Many times during the years following his return to the United States after the war, Donn had said,

"I never want to get old and I want to die in a plane."

He got his wish.

---

102 John Gillespie Magee was killed December 11, 1941, at age 19, just three months after he wrote and sent this poem to his parents.
103 Donn's headstone in Pajaro Valley Memorial Park Cemetery in Watsonville, California

Credits:

- ➤ Behind Barbed Wire — This book, published by and for the prisoners of Stalag Luft I, was distributed only to the men in the camp. All photos and excerpts from this book used by permission, Bauhan Publishing (Richard R. Smith Co/William L. Bauhan, Inc.

- ➤ Tunnel Escape Attempt — From the memoirs of 1st Lt. Robert P. Bird, one of Donn's cellmates at Stalag Luft I. The account of their tunnel escape attempt is reproduced in this book with permission from Robert P. Bird's son, Sheldon.

- ➤ Photo of snow in hills of Italy in winter used with permission from Dreamstime ift.tt/1Ng353X

- ➤ War Stamp images are in the Public Domain via Wikipedia.

- ➤ Posters and photographs depicting WWII — Those used in this book are all in the public domain unless otherwise labeled.

- ➤ Poems — All the poems in this book are by anonymous writers, except for "High Flight" by Pilot Officer John Gillespie Magee, They are all in the public domain, including "High Flight."

- ➤ Government Declassified Documents are in the public domain — including the map depicting the place where Donn's plane was last seen before he was shot down and also the Reparation Reports of Lt. Col. John G. Bright and 2nd Lt. Ed Hyland.

- ➤ The 1st Fighter Group that Donn was in during the war still exists today. Image of an echelon and the photo of guns being loaded in a P-38 are in the public domain and are also used with permission from the 1st Fighter Group webmaster.

- ➤ Special thanks to Verla's granddaughter, Mikayla, for the photo of her in a pair of nylon stockings with seams.

- ➤ All other newspaper clippings, diary entries, letters, personal photographs, etc. are original and are in the possession of Donn's daughter, Verla Kay.

Author's Note:

This story has been a real challenge to compile because there were very few people I could talk to and ask questions of. As the only surviving member of my immediate family, I felt compelled to share my father's story with the world before it was lost forever.

But it wasn't an easy task, because Donn's War Log, the newspaper clippings, books, flight training "yearbooks" and photographs that make up most of the images in this book were hidden away in a storage box that didn't surface until both of my parents were dead. While those bits and pieces of his life during WWII told a really compelling story, there were huge gaps that seemed impossible to fill.

It took over 15 years to bridge those gaps, but fill them in I did. It was all but a miracle when I was talking to one of my cousins (Donn's sister's daughter) about my desire to tell Donn's story and I said, "I just wish I had letters from that time to help tell his story." Sheryl immediately said, "I have a huge packet of letters that your father wrote to Grandma and Grandpa (his parents) during the war. Grandma kept all of them and after she died I didn't know what to do with them, so I stored them away. I'll send them to you."

What a treasure that packet was! It not only contained all of the letters that I've included in this book, but also Donn's "Makeshift Flight Diary," in which he told, in his own words, about some of his missions and what it felt like to be a fighter pilot during the war.

I still had almost no details about his imprisonment in Italy or about his escape before he was captured by the Germans. A chance contact via the internet one day put me in touch with Dennis H. Hill, who was also a prisoner in Italy during the war. Dennis discovered the name of the prison camp my father was in, and also the reparation reports of two men that escaped with my father, which supplied the missing details of Donn's Italian imprisonment, his escape and how he hid in the hills of Italy until he was recaptured by the Germans.

Another internet contact was with the son of one of the men who roomed with my father in the same cell in Stalag Luft I, in Barth, Germany. Sheldon Bird very graciously supplied me with a copy of his father's diary account of the tunnel attempt that my father participated in, giving me an actual account of that event to put in the book. All my father had ever said about it was, "We tried to tunnel out, but we didn't make it."

Through sheer perseverance, I eventually located the current copyright holder of a book my father had, "Behind Barbed Wire." It was published in 1946, by the men in the camp, for the men in the camp and was distributed only to the men in Stalag Luft I prison camp. Sarah Bauhan and Ian Aldrich of the Bauhan Publishing Company gave me permission to use photos and excerpts from that book — which filled out "the rest of Donn's story."

I am extremely pleased to finally be able to share my father's story with the world. He was a wonderful man, strict, honest, caring, loving and full of a real love of life. He had a great sense of humor — I remember him dressing up in a tutu, tights and ballet slippers to participate in a "show" at the Elks Club one night. My mother's sense of humor was just as great. When a fellow crop duster stayed at our house one week to help my father with his overload of work, she first short-sheeted the flyer's bed, then put brush rollers (very prickly) into his bed. But he got even with her. On the last night of his stay, when my mother poured a box filled with dirt clods into her sink full of dirty dishes, thinking it was her dish soap, she laughed until she cried.

Donn was very well known and was beloved by many people in town. When he died, his funeral was one of the largest anyone in town had ever seen. People completely filled the church and overflowed into much of the parking lot outside. The line of cars going from the church to the cemetery was miles long — as far as the eye could see and further.

I was very lucky to have had such a wonderful man for a father, even if it was for such a short time. I was thirteen when he died.

Thank you for letting me share his story with you. I hope you find it as interesting as I have.

About the Author and this Book

Verla Kay is Donn's second daughter. She was married right after high school to Terry Bradley, who also lived in Watsonville, California. She and her husband have been married for over 55 years. They currently have four children, four grandchildren and five great grandchildren. They live in eastern Washington, very close to the Idaho border in a tiny little town of under 500 people. Most of their family is close to them and they are very happy.

Verla loves writing, cooking, playing computer games that have lots of puzzles in them to be solved, and playing board, dice and card games (especially pinochle) with her family and friends.

She has previously had eleven historical picture books in rhyme published, ten of them by Putnam, and one with a small press. This is her first self-published book and it is radically different from her previously published books. **Visit Verla at https://verlakay.com**

Wings Forever took over 15 years to complete. Verla first tried writing Donn's story as a picture book in rhyme, then as scrap-booked pages, and again as two different novels (one in Donn's point of view and then in Norma's). She also tried writing it as purely non-fiction for middle graders, then for high school students and once again for adults. This final version of the book is a compilation of all three of her non-fiction versions. She finally realized that the only way she could truly tell Donn's story was to keep it totally factual, using the vast array of raw material that he and Norma had left behind in their scrapbooks, diaries, letters, newspaper clippings, photographs, etc. It is filled with footnotes and extra explanations of words and terms that today's kids might not find familiar, as it is her hope that some of these young people will read this book and learn what a fighter pilot's life was really like during WWII and how much those brave men sacrificed for all of us.

The cover was created by Verla, using a photograph of the sky and clouds that she took from her back yard. Donn is flying the P-38 on the cover. She PhotoShopped her mother's name (Norma) onto the gondola of the plane, just the way Donn described it in one of his letters to his parents.

This book truly was a labor of love and Verla hopes you have enjoyed it.

Addendum:

This page from Donn's Pilot Log show a few of the missions he flew
during the war and, as you can see, there was a two year gap in the dates
where he — "bailed out on fire." That's when he was shot down and then
was a prisoner of war.

CPSIA information can be obtained
at www.ICGtesting.com
Printed in the USA
LVHW020005081121
702717LV00006B/62

9 780971 790520